CHRIS WATTERS

D0192175

THE
GAMER'S
BUCKET LIST

THE 50 VIDEO GAMES TO PLAY BEFORE YOU DIE

FOREWORD BY:
Stuttering Craig Skistimas of

SCREWATTACK

ISBN 978-1-63353-131-4

From pixelated pioneer adventures to stunning space odysseys, the boundaries of the video game world are expanding every day. Grand epics and gritty mysteries. Fierce competition and friendly cooperation. Powerful emotions and uproarious laughter. Video games are fantastically diverse and wonderfully creative, but not all games are created equal. With so many games out there on so many different consoles, computers, and devices, how do you decide which games are worth playing? Backed by years of writing about games professionally and decades spent playing them, Chris Watters lays out a list of 50 games to entertain and enlighten you. Whether you're trying to learn more about the world of gaming or strengthening your claim to true gaming fluency, these are the games you'll want to play, and why you'll want to play them.

SCREW ATTACK

"Thank you to Craig and the entire Screw Attack team for all their help. It was an honor having you guys provide the foreword to this book."

Chris Watters, Author

Foreword

"Stuttering" Craig Skistimas
ScrewAttack Founder

Whether you're a professional gamer or a mom who enjoys a few
minutes with the latest free-to-play money sucker, it's crazy to think
how much video games impact our lives on a day-to-day basis.
For me, I'm lucky enough to have made working in the video game
industry my life. I've seen video games evolve at an amazing pace,
to the point that they are accessible anywhere at any given time. It's
truly a wonderful thing.

There's a thought that to be an "expert" in something you have to
know everything about a subject. Let me tell you this: there is no way
to know everything about every video game. Too many come out in
any given year and just like other forms of media, everyone tends to
gravitate towards the genres that they prefer. Having a guide to fill
you in on the games that you should check out would be really useful,
wouldn't it? Right? Right. And so here you are, ready to discover and
celebrate some of the best games ever made.

At ScrewAttack, we'd like to think we appreciate all games - even
the bad ones. Ok, MOST of the bad ones. Sure, we have our favorite
genres and games that we love to play, but one thing I've learned is
that you can't pigeonhole yourself into only liking one type of game.
Being diverse and well-rounded in your gaming selection is crucial.
It's almost like video games are a metaphor for life or something!
With that said, you may find some of your favorite games in this
book; others, you may have never even heard of. The games that
Chris chronicles in this book may not have been the most popular
in terms of sales, but they're all important for establishing a picture
of where video games are today, and giving you an idea of what is
in store for the future. Whether this book ends up on a bookshelf,
a coffee table, or a toilet, I hope you enjoy taking your time and
learning what makes these games so great. Happy reading from your
friends at ScrewAttack.

" We are all going to die. You can't avoid it. But you can chose how you go. Outside, in the sunshine, like some sort of animal, or inside your darkened living room, playing games? If you want to get through the 50 excellent games in this book, then the choice is clear. "

Tim Schafer, President and CEO of Double Fine Productions

" With thousands of games released each and every year, trying to figure out what you need to play is daunting. In The Gamer's Bucket List, Chris gives anyone with a passing interest a comprehensive list of the games they need to play paired with the wit and passion that has made him an industry veteran. Although Patapon 3's absence from the list is disturbing. *"*

Greg Miller, Co-Founder of KindaFunny.com

DEDICATION

To the family who brought games into my life and taught me moderation, to the friends who left doors ajar and couch seats open so I could play with them, to the coworkers who matched wits and wrangled words and made video magic with me and to the partner who supports me and inspires me and threatens to beat me at Tetris (and does).

Contents

Introduction

Chris Watters
Author

As you read through this book, odds are you will reach a moment when you wonder, "Why isn't such-and-such game in here?!" Though I've made this list full to the bursting with some of the best games ever made, I had to impose some limitations, as much for the sake of the book as for my own sanity.

The most notable of these boundaries is the online realm. I've spent countless hours relishing the triumphs and tribulations of online multiplayer play, but such experiences are, by their very nature, fleeting. Though titans like World of Warcraft and Counter-Strike continue to draw crowds more than a decade on from their original releases, there are hundreds of other online worlds and arenas whose time has come and gone. If online multiplayer is the primary mode in which a game excels, I've left it out of the book in the interest of creating a list that will stand the test of time. Or at least, hold out a bit longer.

In addition to doing what future-proofing I can, I've endeavored to cast the net wide to encompass a broad range of gaming experiences. Some are exactly as you imagine them, while others might not be what you'd expect. I encourage you to give them all a try, because in each there is a spark capable of igniting a passion for the deeply creative, wonderfully diverse, and downright awesome world of video games.

Oh, and one more thing. Paring down the list was hard enough; ordering it was impossible. The games are arranged randomly, with the exception of Spelunky, which I put first because it is my favorite (Being the author has its perks, after all).

If you'd like to talk about game you found in here, ask me politely about a game you didn't, or generally chat about all things video games, you can reach me on Twitter at @CTWatters. Now get busy reading, or get busy playing. Preferably both.

PRESS START

1-10*

Spelunky

First Released **Jul 4, 2012**

When you first venture into the caverns of Spelunky, you may smile at the first snake that sedately slithers towards you, waiting to be dispatched with your trusty whip. You may puff up with confidence the first time you use a bomb to blast yourself a handy shortcut. "I'm a regular Indiana Jones," you might think to yourself, "I got this." This two-dimensional platformer can seem welcoming with its cartoonish characters and lighthearted vibe, but you'll soon learn the truth. A snake isn't so sedate when it's hiding a jar to ambush you, and a bomb can kill you as easily as help you. Runaway boulders move a lot faster in Spelunky than in the movies, and you most definitely do not "got this."

You will die. A lot. Sometimes you'll laugh at your misfortune, other times you will rage. You may survive for minutes upon minutes, or you may die in a matter of seconds. Spikes, arrow traps, exploding frogs, carnivorous plants, lava people, yetis, vampires, crocodile men, and more all wait to claim your life, and claim it they shall. Over and over and over again.

But with each death, you learn. The levels change when you die and you begin each attempt with the same starter kit of items, so you have a clean slate and new caverns to face with each new life. The only difference between your 1st playthrough and your 401st playthrough is the knowledge and skill you have earned. You come to realize that your tens, hundreds, thousands of deaths have not been separate attempts, but rather one continuous struggle to become the savvy, heroic, dashing adventurer that part of you has always dreamed of being. And that's the true brilliance of Spelunky; it doesn't give you amazing skills and say, "Here, you're an adventurer now. Have fun!" Spelunky gives you an amazing world and says, "So, you wanna be an adventurer? Prove it."

GO TO HELL

Spelunky has many secrets, chief among them the hidden sequence of feats you must perform to reach the secret bonus levels and conquer the true final boss. Beating it normally is just the beginning.

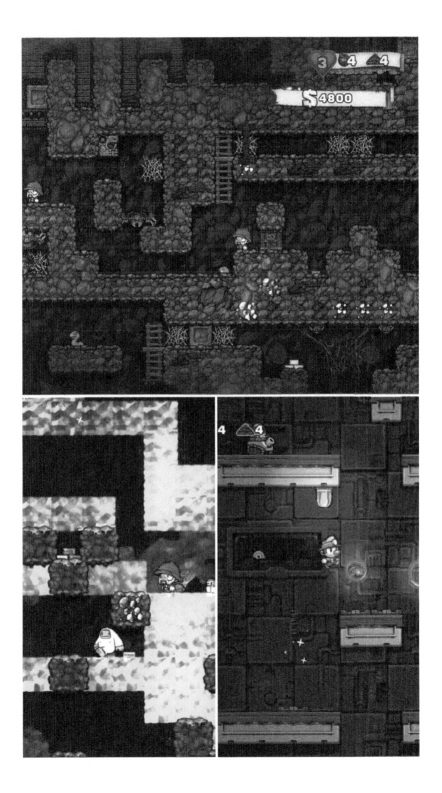

Assassin's Creed II

PS3, PC, X360, MAC   First Released **Nov 17, 2009**

There are few franchises in video games as adept at transporting you to another time in history as Assassin's Creed. From the Holy Land during the Crusades to the Caribbean during the Golden Age of Piracy, Assassin's Creed games excel at bringing places to life, and nowhere is this more evident than in the magnificent Assassin's Creed II. The cities and countryside of Renaissance-era Italy are the subjects here, rendered in such loving detail and astonishing complexity that a simple stroll down the street is enough to dazzle you. It's well worth taking a brief respite from your century-spanning struggle between powerful secret societies for the fate of humanity to stop and smell the roses.

But don't tarry too long, because as Ezio Auditore da Firenze, you've got a lot to do. There are secrets to ferret out and mysteries to uncover and Templars to kill, and not necessarily in that order. Though the story follows a set path, you are often free to carry out missions as you see fit. You may rely on stealth, blending in with the crowd in the bustling piazzas of Florence and knifing a target with your spring-loaded hidden blades. You might choose speed, clambering up the side of a building and racing across rooftops to escape unwanted attention. Or you could use brute force, elegantly dodging and parrying the attacks of numerous guards as you cut them down one by one.

There's an elegance to all of Ezio's actions that make it a thrill to don his hooded robes, and unraveling his connections with the modern-day protagonist, Desmond, is an exciting and gratifying endeavor. Characters with character, cities with soul, action with style, and conspiracies with depth all combine to make Assassin's Creed II an incredible adventure.

Dead Space

PC, X360, PS3   First Released **Oct 13, 2008**

To play a video game is to give up some control over your emotional state. No matter how stoic you may try to remain in the face of fast-paced action, witty dialogue, dramatic storytelling, or plaintive music, some part of you is feeling what that game wants you to feel, providing that game is any good at what it does. Dead Space is very, very good at what it does, and what it wants you to feel is nerve-fraying, gut-churning, heart-pounding terror.

To accomplish this goal, Dead Space uses all the tricks in the horror book and then some. The game is set on a large spaceship overrun with gruesomely mutated humanoid creatures. These monsters are terrifying to behold, and even the sound of one scuttling through the walls is enough to set your skin crawling. The sound effects and musical cues in Dead Space are impeccably designed to draw you deeper into the experience, and as they echo through the oppressive, claustrophobic corridors of the spaceship, you may be tempted to yell at the screen, "Don't go in there!" But this isn't a horror movie; you are in control. You are the one that is going in there, and that makes it all the more frightening.

Fortunately, you are not defenseless, and the arsenal of repurposed mining tools that you use to fight back is formidable. The creatures don't die easily, so you'll have to take time to dismember them instead of just blowing them away, and this ingenious system heightens the tension of combat. The story of your mission to figure out what's going on and evacuate survivors is a harrowing one, suffused with dread and punctuated by some jaw-dropping action sequences (did someone say zero gravity?). Dead Space is a master class in horror, destined to claw its way into your mind and never, ever leave.

The Last of Us REMASTERED

PS4   First Released **July 29, 2014**

What really happens when it all goes to hell? In The Last of Us, a pandemic has turned most of humanity into vicious creatures and the survivors, like the cities they shelter in, are ruins of their former selves. It's a beautiful, richly detailed world that tells the story of how badly something can be broken, and how hard it can be to mend. The two lead characters represent both sides of this coin: Joel, the gruff, unkind guardian whom you play as, and Ellie, the guarded, headstrong teenager that you must guide across the wild country. Their fraught, tender relationship is the driving force of this game, and you'll find yourself rapt with attention to see how their journey ends.

Playing the guardian isn't easy, however. In addition to the vicious mutants that stalk you, there are packs of bandits that survive by taking what they want by force. Indeed, combat in The Last of Us is forceful and violent, and though a stealthy approach is often best, there are many times when brutal melee attacks or loud gunfire are your only recourse. Fights have a hard-edged intensity that is both stressful and gratifying.

You simply must play the remastered version of this game because it includes Left Behind, and these extra chapters are a paragon of video game storytelling. Playing as Ellie, you venture just outside of your walled city with your friend, Riley, in the post-apocalyptic version of a day at the mall. Participating in their teenage mischief involves some sublimely inventive gameplay, and the dialogue and character performances are utterly captivating. Even if you've already been playing them for years and years, Left Behind is the kind of experience that makes you fall in love with video games all over again.

Portal 2

PC, X360, MAC, PS3   First Released **Apr 18, 2011**

The story of a woman with a portal gun and an artificial intelligence with a sadistic sense of humor first captured our imaginations in Portal, a spectacular, if short, game released in 2007. By shooting this gun at one surface and then another, you could create two oval-shaped portals. Walk in one and you come out the other. Jump off of a ledge into one and fly out the other. Put one on the floor, one on the ceiling above it, and you can fall forever. Playing around with the portal gun was great fun, and using it to solve the tricky puzzles was very satisfying. Tie it all together with an A.I. guide that slowly transitions from innocuous instructor to malevolent manipulator, and you've got a lovely little game.

Portal 2, then, is this lovely little game blown out in every direction to make a sequel that is bigger, brainier, and more bizarrely hilarious than its predecessor. The small test chambers open up to a sprawling scientific complex, packed with outlandish new discoveries and plenty of portal puzzles. There's a cooperative mode, so you can team up with someone else to take on even tougher puzzles with twice as many portals.

And then there's the writing. Portal 2 has some of the most sublimely funny writing ever to grace a video game. From the ambitiously maniacal founder of this strange science facility to the sophisticated A.I.'s that vie for your loyalty to the demented talking machinery you must wrangle, there are perhaps more quotable lines in Portal 2 than in any other game. These characters aren't just comic relief either; they are sympathetic and nuanced and genuinely intriguing. (Yes, even the spherical one that just yells about space most of the time.) You'll laugh, you'll cheer, you'll have a fantastic time, and you'll never volunteer for a scientific study ever again.

A.I.'S SAY THE DARNDEST THINGS

Okay, fine. Let's all act like humans. 'Look at me. Boy, do I love sweating. Let's convert beef and leaves into energy and excrete them later and go shopping.'

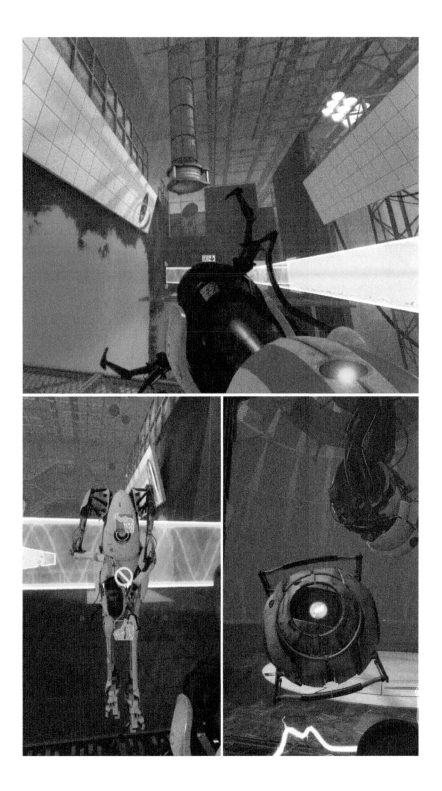

Mass Effect 2

PC, X360, PS3   First Released **Jan 26, 2010**

Okay, this is a weird one. The Mass Effect trilogy is a tremendous achievement, a sweeping space opera that takes place in a universe so richly imagined that it rivals titans like Star Wars and Star Trek for sheer narrative potential. So why select Mass Effect 2? Why not just start with Mass Effect and carry your character through the whole trilogy? Well, hopefully that's what you'll do, because it's a grand, awe-inspiring journey. This book is a bucket list, however, and if there's one game from this series you simply can't miss, it's the crown jewel, Mass Effect 2.

You play as Commander Shepard (gender, hairstyle, and facial features chosen by you), a heroic human space captain in a future in which humanity has recently emerged on a galactic stage populated by fascinating alien races. Faced with an overwhelming threat from deep space, you must recruit a multicultural crew that is ready to lay down their lives for the fate of all organic life. The combat is exciting, thanks to your powerful mix of guns and space magic (that's not a technical term), but it's the relationships that make Mass Effect 2 so special.

Relationships are fueled by choices, large and small. As you choose responses in the game's frequent conversations, you mold your own version of Shepard. Though you take ownership of her decisions and actions, you're more of a guide than a ventriloquist. Shepard has her own personality as well, and this makes playing the role of the Commander much more engaging. And then there's your crew, a diverse cast of some of the most memorable characters in all of video games. Conversing with them is a reward unto itself, and the bonds you form with them won't soon be forgotten. Mass Effect 2 is a marvel of grand-scale drama made personal, the emotional high water mark in a captivating series.

A SCI-FI MAJOR GENERAL

Just because it's a space opera, doesn't mean there is singing. But there is singing in Mass Effect 3, and it's a fantastic Gilbert & Sullivan cameo.

Gone Home

PC, MAC   First Released **Aug 15, 2013**

A girl comes home from college. Her parents are out for the evening, and her sister has left a note, asking her not to investigate where she has gone. The girl explores the house, looking for clues to her sister's whereabouts. That's it.

That's... it? Well, yes, in a way. There are no alternate places to visit, enemies to fight, puzzles to solve, or conversations to navigate. Many of the elements you'd commonly associate with video games are absent from Gone Home, and this is part of what makes it special. Video games are a constantly evolving art form, and decades after the first ones gained mainstream popularity, we are still seeing new games that push the boundaries in exciting and intriguing ways.

Gone Home is such a game, but it didn't earn a spot in this book on the strength of novelty alone. As you explore the house, you learn a little bit about who you are: a college student named Kaitlin, come home after a year abroad to the house her family moved into while she was away. You, like Kaitlin, don't really know what mom, dad, and lil' sis have been up to, but as you find letters, diaries, books, photos, and notes of all kinds, you begin to weave together the tapestry of your family's life.

You read about your father's work struggles, your mother's loneliness, and most poignantly of all, your sister's growing friendship with a new girl at school. The rooms in which you find these scraps are rich with details, and the subtlety and humanity of the writing is astonishing. By the end, you don't just feel like you know these people, you feel like you understand them in a meaningful way. This is called empathy, and that a video game can so powerfully channel this deep human feeling is remarkable indeed.

Journey

PS3, PS4   First Released **Mar 13, 2012**

The artistic diversity of video games is staggering, as befits any medium with countless passionate creators. The artistry of Journey, however, is particularly wonderful. You play as a cloaked figure wandering in the desert, through the ruins and remnants of a long lost civilization, with your eyes on a distant mountaintop. The warm earth tones of your robe both contrast and blend with the pale sparkling sands of the desert. Hues and shades change as you press onward, but it seems that you could pause the game at any moment and be looking a beautiful image.

Journey's artistry is not merely visual. As you trudge up sand dunes and glide down them, there is beauty in your movement. Your flowing robe and fluttering scarf trace a graceful silhouette, so don't be surprised to find yourself frolicking about just because it feels so good. It's a rare game that can make merely moving around a joyful experience, but Journey is just such a game.

There is beauty, too, in Journey's solitude and companionship. For much of the game, you travel alone, a solitary figure amidst ageless mysteries. But suddenly, you are not alone. An anonymous player has joined you, and though you can only communicate through chimes, you are drawn together by your shared endeavor. How your adventure together takes shape is yet another mystery, one you can only solve by playing through to the end. Journey is a resonant and resplendent adventure, not to be missed.

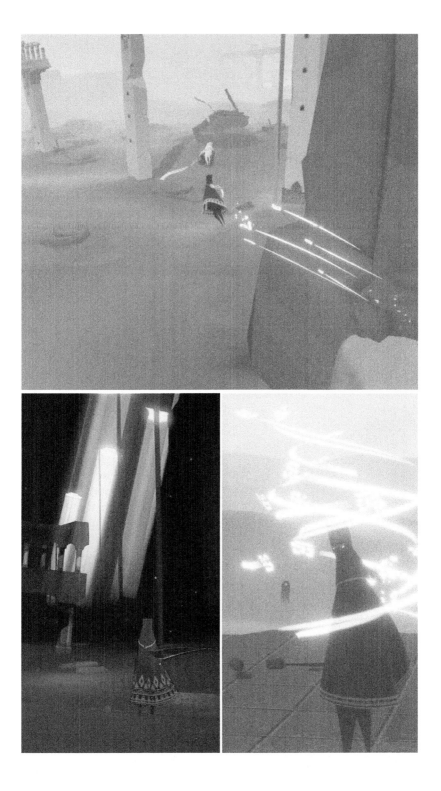

Red Dead Redemption

X360, PS3   First Released **May 18, 2010**

Red Dead Redemption is the greatest Western that the video game industry has ever produced. That alone should get it on your bucket list, but if you need a little more convincing or just want to know what you have to look forward to, read on.

You play as John Marston, an outlaw-gone-clean forced to get dirty again when government agents kidnap his family and demand that he hunt down his former partners-in-crime. Marston's long and winding quest is full of eccentric allies and nasty enemies who lend the narrative much of its juicy Western flavor.

Like many a stoic gunslinger before him, Marston didn't get to be the man he is by talking. The gunfights you get into are varied and plentiful; from racing across the chaparral on horseback to taking cover behind the bar in a saloon to leaping from car to car on the back of a moving train. Red Dead Redemption is packed with exciting moments that bring the outlaw fantasy to life, but thankfully, it's not all gunplay. There's plenty of time to ride across the open range and see what adventures await.

You might go on the hunt for valuable plants or animal pelts; just be sure a cougar doesn't make you its prey. You might find a stranger desperate for help; just be sure that her overturned cart isn't hiding an ambush. Red Dead Redemption's world is a dangerous one, but it's also beautiful. When you see the sun setting over a broad bend in the river with the dusty hills rolling off into the distance, you can't help but stop and stare a while. With the Wild West stretching out in front of you and the fantastic soundtrack setting the mood, this game is a living room cowboy's dream come true.

WHOA THERE!

Marston's lasso is one of the stars of the show, whether you're roping and taming a wild horse, running down a man with a bounty on his head, or dragging an ornery varmint behind your horse as you trot through a cactus patch.

Uncharted 2:
Among Thieves

PS3   First Released **October 13, 2009**

Of all the high-flying action movie heroes that video games have produced, Nathan Drake is the best. The star of the Uncharted series is handsome, charming, witty, and fueled by just the right cocktail of decency and rakishness. But he wouldn't be such an appealing character if he didn't have such an excellent supporting cast, and Sully, Elena, and Chloe aren't simply one-dimensional foils. They burst with life onto the screen, excellently acted and wonderfully animated, enriching every scene they are in and making the story of Uncharted 2 a pleasure to unravel.

It is the story of a treasure hunt that takes on grave importance as you discover the truth about the object you seek. Powerful items attract powerful enemies, and Drake is a skilled fighter. You can brandish guns and sling grenades with gusto, but you're no bullet sponge. You must be nimble to outfox your aggressive pursuers, flitting from cover to cover and clambering around the environment to get a better position. Like all good action heroes, Drake can throw a punch, and finishing off an enemy in hand-to-hand combat is particularly satisfying.

A globe-trotting blockbuster wouldn't be complete without breathtaking locations, and Uncharted 2 is a traveler's dream come true (but with slightly, make that vastly, more peril). From ornate museums to deep jungles to war-torn cities to mountaintop temples, the environments are dazzlingly beautiful; don't resist the urge to stop and stare. And when events come to a climax in one of the many dramatic set pieces, Uncharted 2 cements its place among the best games of all time. The train scene. The tank scene. The hotel scene. The village scene. These moments are ensconced in video game canon for good reason, and you simply must experience them for yourself.

LOADING...

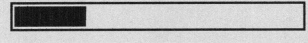

11-20

Nidhogg

PC, PS4, MAC, VITA   First Released **Jan 13, 2014**

A duel. A fight to the death. Human conflict distilled into its purest form. The popularity of duels has ebbed and flowed over the course of history, but the very nature of one-on-one combat still speaks to us in a primal way. In a base, brutal voice, a duel challenges us to prove our superiority over another, to prove our own bravery to ourselves, and to prove ourselves worthy of sacrifice to the great worm god.

Okay, so technically Nidhogg is a serpent from Norse mythology. If you take umbrage at the joke, then perhaps a duel is in order? Because that's what Nidhogg is–Duel: The Game–and it sets the stage perfectly. Two 2D silhouettes face off, swords in hand. The few attack options and movement abilities you have are easy to execute, which makes the barrier to entry feel invitingly low. Once combat begins, however, death can come swiftly. If your opponent lands a single thrust of her sword, your body will crumble to the ground as brightly-colored pixels spurt out of your brightly-colored body in a fountain of fluorescent death.

But death is not the end. Once you are slain, your opponent has the advantage and is free to run toward the sacrificial altar where victory awaits a few screens over. You, however, will soon appear in her way again, and should you slay her in turn, the advantage is now yours. So long as you have it, slipping past your opponent can be just as effective as slicing through her, and with evasion as effective as elimination, each encounter escalates exquisitely. Nidhogg is one of those beautiful games in which simplicity gives rise to complexity in perfect proportion, but it never feels so complicated that you are hopelessly outclassed. Everyone has a fighting chance in Nidhogg, so go ahead. Challenge someone to a duel.

Psychonauts

XBOX, PC, PS2, MAC   First Released **Apr 19, 2005**

Playing Psychonauts is like letting yourself in on a juicy secret. Whenever you think about it, you get a big, self-satisfied grin on your face and when you meet someone else who is in the know, you can't help but squeal with shared excitement. This is a game that will bring joy into your life as you play it, and for years afterwards. It's your classic kid-joins-summer-camp-for-the-psychically-gifted-and-adventures-inside-the-minds-of-weirdos-to-unravel-conspiracy tale, but you've never played one quite like this.

You play as Raz, a kid with psychic powers who runs away from the circus to do normal kid things like attend summer camp. At said camp he meets a bunch of other kids like him, as well as the adult counselors who are there to train the lil' whippersnappers in the ways of telekinesis, invisibility, pyrokinesis, levitation, and other such powers. Using your abilities to solve puzzles is a lot of fun largely because the situations you have to put them to work in are wonderfully creative. You may never play another game with levels as clever and inventive as those in Psychonauts.

You'll enter a paranoid psyche and find yourself in a bizarre recreation of 1950s American suburbia in which every husband and housewife is a poorly disguised, suit-wearing secret agent. You'll play a board game while shrunk to the size of a game piece and stomp around a city of fish-people as a towering giant. And all the while you'll be smiling, giggling, or laughing hysterically at the hilarious dialogue. Psychonauts has a dazzling sense of humor accompanied by an undercurrent of empathy for those who face larger-than-life mental demons; it's compassion and comedy in beautiful harmony. And when it's all over, you'll head straight to the Internet to look up quotes to prepare for when you meet someone who has also played this very special game.

Superbrothers:
Sword & Sworcery EP

iOS, PC, MAC   First Released **Mar 24, 2011**

Long gone are the days when mobile games were synonymous with match-3 clones and uninspired dreck. Sure, there are still lots of match-3 clones and uninspired dreck, but there are also beautiful, resonant games like Superbrothers: Sword & Sworcery EP. It's an adventure game in which you guide a hero on a quest through a strange land to find magical artifacts, but it's presented by a suited figure in a chair who addresses you directly and shares quips like, "You woke the deathless specter who still lurks in the darkness beneath Mingi Taw. What a creep, amirite?" It's a classic premise cast in modern sensibilities with an unforgettable sense of style.

A lot of that style comes from the gorgeous art. Though it's mostly squared edges and small blocks, the delicate artistry makes it feel like a pointillistic painting. There are luminous forests, foreboding monuments, pristine pools, and echoing caverns that inspire awe no matter what size screen you play it on. Accompanying these sights are the pitch-perfect sounds that give your mythical explorations just a bit more grandeur and infuse the rhythmic combat with some extra gravitas. And the impeccable soundtrack sets the mood just right; it's somewhere between playful and pensive, both ethereal and down-to-earth.

These dichotomies extend to the writing as well. In your grave sojourn to retrieve items of great power, you enlist the help of a woodsman named Logfella and his dog, Dogfella. Superbrothers' sense of humor and self-awareness blends beautifully with its reverence of nature; the game will just as soon suggest you tweet a line of dialogue as ask you to observe the phases of the moon above you (like, the actual moon). It's a game of contrasts that feels both familiar and altogether new, an immensely creative and inspiring adventure that you don't want to miss.

Super Meat Boy

X360, MAC, PC, PS4, VITA   First Released **Oct 20, 2010**

Casting an Italian plumber as a daring hero who performs death-defying leaps and runs across dangerous landscapes to save a princess isn't what you'd call an obvious choice, but hey, it worked out pretty well. So if a humble tradesman can do it, why not a cube-shaped boy made entirely of raw meat? In Meat Boy's quest to save his heavily bandaged girlfriend from an evil fetus in a jar, he challenges Mario's place on the throne of precision platforming action, and wins.

There are hundreds of levels in Super Meat Boy, but most can be completed in a matter of seconds. This does not mean that you will breeze through the game, however, because after some quick introductory levels, things get very difficult very quickly. Spikes, sawblades, and other deadly traps will pulverize Meat Boy in an instant. Fortunately, you can restart the level just as quickly, so dying is less of a disheartening setback and more of a bump in the road. The going can get rough, but facing these tough challenges yields such sweet rewards.

Super Meat Boy is one of those games that just feels right. As you run, leap, cling to walls, and leap some more, you get in tune with the perfectly calibrated controls. It's easy to appreciate the liquid precision with which you move, and this satisfaction holds fast even when you're frustrated by the obstacles you face. The game feels so good to play that you can't help but have confidence in yourself, and herein lies the balance that makes Super Meat Boy so sublime. It gives you confidence and challenges that confidence in equal measure, so whether you succeed on your 3rd or 73rd attempt, you still feel like a hero.

DARING DUOS

This entire game was created by just two developers! Their creative journey, along with those of some other fascinating game developers, are deftly chronicled in Indie Game: The Movie (which was also made by two people).

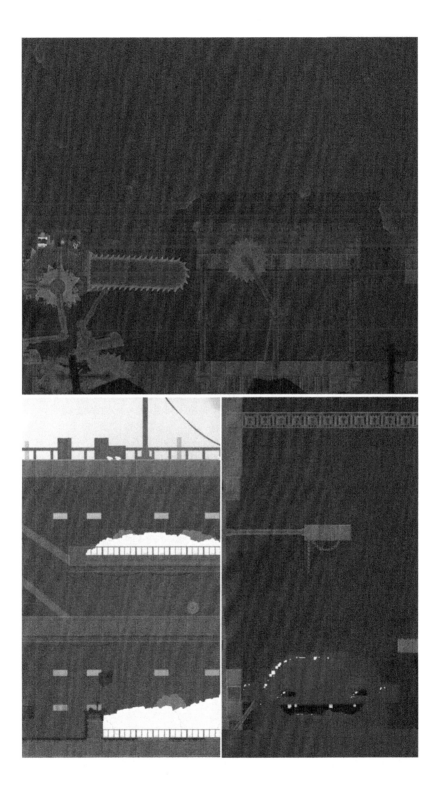

Rock Band 3

X360, PS3, Wii   First Released **Oct 26, 2010**

For a period of time in the late 2000s, rock 'n' roll games ruled the roost. With plastic guitars in hand, players tapped out their stadium-sized dreams on living room-sized stages, strumming along to colored notes that scrolled by on the screen and hearing their button presses blasted back to them as songs they knew and loved. With the addition of microphones and plastic drum sets, players lived the highs and lows of being in a video game band: the thrill of rocking out a killer set, the problem of where to put all of this plastic gear.

Gear may be your greatest obstacle in playing the best game this era produced, Rock Band 3, but don't let that deter you. Track down two guitars, a microphone, and a drum set (be sure they are compatible with your system of choice), and you and your bandmates are in for an unforgettable time. This isn't a game you just play once. This is a game you host parties for or set regular band practices around. Once you're into it, pick up two more mics to unleash some sweet vocal harmony, and hunt down a keyboard to take your band to the next level.

Playing the keyboard and drums can actually teach you some dexterity that may be transferrable if you want to transition to the real thing; for learning guitar, it's better to seek out a more learning-focused game, like Rocksmith. What Rock Band 3 excels at is accessibility. You design your band, take them on tour, and play your way through the 83 song track list featuring too many stellar bands to list here. This is game that brings people together, and then makes those people feel like legendary gods of living room rock.

The Witcher 3: Wild Hunt

PC, XONE, PS4   First Released **May 18, 2015**

Meet Geralt of Rivia. He has a very particular set of skills, skills he has acquired over a very long career. Skills that make him a nightmare for the monsters, spirits, demons, and other supernatural nasties that plague his medieval world. Hunting such creatures for coin is all in a day's work for a witcher, and wielding his powerful combination of swords, potions, and magical signs makes for exciting combat. Turning in the head of a griffin for a reward is satisfying, but the beauty of the Wild Hunt is that it's never quite as simple as all that.

Every contract has a story, and The Witcher 3 is very fond of adding twists and turns that play with your expectations. There are grander stories, too; as Geralt, you find yourself embroiled in the ongoing political struggles of warring nations as you search for your imperiled protégé, enlisting the help of dwarves, sorceresses, crime lords, emperors, and more. Though it is spawned from a series of Polish novels thick with lore, you don't need to know Vizima from Vesemir to get caught up in this game. The Witcher 3 is not encumbered by its literary past, it is enriched by it.

And it all plays out in one of the most incredible open worlds ever created. Not only are the fields and forests of The Witcher 3 beautiful to behold, they are also teeming with treasure to find, gear to craft, enemies to fight, and strange tales to discover. You could spend hours roaming the countryside, totally ignoring the main quests, and still fall in love with this game. But The Witcher 3 is so excellent in so many ways that you won't want to ignore any of it.

GO NATIVE

There are many helpful display items on screen to aid you in better understanding The Witcher 3. Once you're comfortable with what's going on, consider turning them all off to better immerse yourself in this world and appreciate its beauty.

Super Mario World

SNES, GBA, Wii, WiiU   First Released **November 21, 1990**

The plumber, the myth, the legend may have earned his fame well before this first outing on the Super Nintendo, but Super Mario World elevated the brothers Mario to new heights. The power of the new console helped the tried-and-true formula flourish in wonderful ways, from the vibrant visuals and the catchy music, to the ingenious level designs and the introduction of a faithful companion who would become a star in his own right, Yoshi.

In a game full of clever innovations, Yoshi is the standout. Riding on this cheery and capable dinosaur is an absolute delight. He gobbles enemies up and spits them out; he kicks his legs to jump just a bit higher, and crashes down to the earth with a satisfying thump. But though his abilities are a blast to use, it's not just his skills that make him such a special addition to the Mario scene. His cute animations and endearing noises are utterly charming, and sitting in his saddle, you feel like you're off on a grand adventure. Yoshi gives the game heart, and that goes a long way.

Of course, it also helps that the levels are superbly designed, paced in an elegantly increasing difficulty curve and peppered with secrets that are a treat to discover. Each level seems to have some new wrinkle to pique your interest, making you think in a new way or pushing your skills just a bit further. Reaching the jubilant fanfare at the end of each level is the perfect pat on the back, and marking where you've been and charting where you'll go next on the whimsical world map is still satisfying all these decades later. All too often in life, the joys of the past fade over time, but Super Mario World radiates vitality, ingenuity, and exuberance, and that makes it evergreen.

Half-Life 2

PC, MAC, LNX, XBOX, X360, PS3   First Released **November 16, 2004**

"Wake up, Mr. Freeman. Wake up and smell the ashes."

Even if you don't know who Mr. Freeman is or what the deal is with the ashes, the speech at the beginning of Half-Life 2 drips with foreboding. You've woken up on a train pulling into a station. As you disembark, a flying drone snaps your picture and a man on a large video screen welcomes you to City 17, "one of our finest remaining urban centers." So begins the ominous introduction to one of the best first-person shooters of all time.

Atmosphere and setting are two of the most important elements in Half-Life 2, and they are beautifully realized. Half-Life 2 takes place on an occupied Earth, but the alien invaders aren't a monolithic army. Some work with human collaborators to oppress the population, some fight with you in the resistance effort, and some are simply wild creatures that pose a threat to anyone and everyone. This diversity makes the conflict feel grand in scale, and this feeling is compounded by the large environments you explore. Whether you're driving a car along a deserted coastline searching for supplies or picking your way through infested city streets avoiding deadly traps, Half-Life 2 makes you feel like you're finding your own way in a vast, troubled world.

Of course, you have help. The charismatic characters you ally yourself with on the way inspire loyalty and affection, and the weapons you wield give you a satisfying array of explosive ways to express your devotion. The best part of your arsenal is the gravity gun, a brilliant device that lets you pick up any loose object and shoot it out at high speed. Use it to kill foes, to solve puzzles, and to have a little physics-based fun on your journey. Or a lot. As the potential savior of humanity, you owe it to yourself to blow off a little steam, and as an aficionado of awesome video games, you owe it to yourself to play Half-Life 2.

MOST ANTICIPATED

After the release of Half-Life 2's excellent follow-ups, Episodes 1 and 2, the gaming world has waited with bated breath for news of Half-Life 3. As of this publication, the wait continues.

God of War III

PS3, PS4   First Released **Mar 16, 2010**

The thirst for revenge has driven countless violence-fueled fantasies across many forms of media, but no one drinks quite so deeply from the cup of vengeance as Kratos. Betrayed by the gods of ancient Greece, Kratos set out on a franchise-launching quest to kill anyone in the Greek Pantheon he can get his big angry hands on. In God of War III, the core trilogy comes to a spectacular conclusion.

Spectacle is the key word here, because few games make use of scale as well as this one. In the opening sequence, Kratos climbs around on the body of a colossal titan as she herself climbs the towering Mount Olympus in order to strike at the gods. The titan constantly shifts and moves beneath you like a living mountain, but the game handles it perfectly, allowing you to appreciate the immensity of your surroundings while still fighting off vicious foes. But though your enemies can be fierce, none are as brutal as Kratos himself. From hacking chunks of flesh out of the god of the underworld to ripping the eyeball clean out of cyclops' head, Kratos relishes the gruesome, hyper-violent deaths of all who stand in his way. This is a decidedly gory game, and not for the squeamish.

The violence is part of the spectacle, though, and it serves as a barbaric punctuation mark for the fast-paced, fluid combat. Kratos slashes with swinging blades, skewers with flaming arrows, and bludgeons with gauntlets shaped like lions. Getting swept up in this delirious dance of death is brutally satisfying, and the gorgeous visuals and sweeping soundtrack that bring it to life make it all the better. It's good to be a god.

VENGEANCE!
Some gamers may be planning their revenge right now for the choice of God of War III over God of War II. Play the remastered version in God of War Collection and choose for yourself.

StarCraft II:
Wings of Liberty

PC, MAC   First Released **Jul 27, 2010**

Whoever said war was good for absolutely nothing must have never played a video game. There are legions of great games depicting the myriad facets of war from different perspectives, from the soldiers who meet in battle and the refugees who are displaced by conflict, to the diplomats who pit nations against each other and the generals who command their forces. This latter angle is particularly fertile ground for the real-time strategy genre, and the reigning king of that realm is StarCraft II.

Wings of Liberty is the first of the three installments of StarCraft II, the one that puts you in control of the Terran species. Since StarCraft's debut in 1998, its signature structure has featured three playable species: the Terran, humans who fight inside heavily armored suits; the Protoss, vaguely humanoid aliens with scientifically advanced units; and the Zerg, freaky mutant aliens that reproduce at an alarming rate. Each species is intricately designed to look menacing and powerful, making for battlefields that bristle with vivid details.

And the battlefield is where StarCraft II shines. In most missions you start with basic units and then proceed to harvest resources and construct buildings that allow you to grow your army. You then use this army to destroy your opponents, but from this basic structure blossoms an incredible range of strategies. Even within a given species, there are many ways to approach a given challenge; the sheer variety of viable tactics among all three species is staggering. StarCraft II's brilliance lies in the fact that though its complexity makes for thrilling high-level competitive play, the satisfaction of planning and executing a successful campaign is accessible to everybody. There is room in these ranks for commanders of all skill levels, and those who enlist can be confident they are signing on with the best in the business.

LOADING...

21 - 30

Minecraft

WEB, PC, MAC, PS4, PS3, VITA, X360, XONE   First Released **May 17, 2009**

From a single designer to a multi-billion dollar business, the story of Minecraft's massive popularity is mighty impressive. To have that kind of success, you have to reach an astonishing number of pooplo, and the number of avenues by which people have found their way to Minecraft is remarkable. You can play Minecraft on just about any device that has or can be hooked up to a screen. You can watch people play Minecraft live at any hour of the day. You can buy Minecraft toys, wear Minecraft clothes, and go to Minecon, the official Minecraft convention. You can even read about it in books.

As prevalent as they are, the number of ways you can engage with Minecraft is dwarfed by the number of things you can do in Minecraft. The game puts you in a vast open world in which everything is made out of cubes. Blocky trees grow beside blocky rivers and blocky hills roll off towards distant blocky mountains. Every bit of this landscape can be harvested for crafting materials which you can then use to make anything your heart desires, such as armor and weapons for fighting aggressive creatures, building materials to make structures, food to fill your blocky belly, and mechanisms to fulfill various purposes.

And oh, what purposes these blocks can be put to! The survival mode can challenge you to think creatively, but you can also leave the monsters behind, fly through the air, and create freely. From designing spaceships to staging operas to building working computers within the game, the list of things people have used Minecraft to create is mind-blowing. Whether you're playing alone or joining others online, Minecraft is a marvel of creative potential, an incredible sandbox in which the only limits are your imagination!

...okay, that was a super cheesy ending, but seriously, this game is incredible.

Tetris

COMPUTERS, CONSOLES, PHONES, ET CETERA   First Released **June 6, 1984**

For many of you reading this book, this one's a gimme. You've played it on your computer, your console, your calculator, your phone, or pretty much anything with a screen and some inputs. It's a well-traveled classic, but this evergreen Russian puzzler is just as excellent as it was when it first marched passed the Iron Curtain and into home computers around the world.

Your task is simple, but impossible. Blocks fall from the top of the screen. You steer and rotate the blocks to fit them together, trying to complete solid horizontal lines across the playing field to clear blocks in order to keep the screen from filling up. It's easy at first, but the blocks begin to fall faster and faster and soon one small mistake can spell disaster. There's no "beating" Tetris; there's only the struggle to push your score a little higher, to hold out a little longer. Consequently, there's no end to Tetris, and you can never truly be done with it. It may be minutes between games or years, but once you've got those blocks rotating in your head, they're there to stay.

Tetris is its purest form may be the closest to perfect a video game has ever been, but that doesn't mean there aren't some great variations on the theme. Many console versions of the game (notably The New Tetris for Nintendo 64) include head-to-head modes in which clearing lines deposits extra blocks on your opponent's playing field and makes them want to curse your name unto the heavens. And for a more mind-bending take on the classic, try Welltris, in which the pieces fall down the walls of a four-sided well and you try to make lines on the bottom. This one's out of Lassie's league, so you're on your own, comrade.

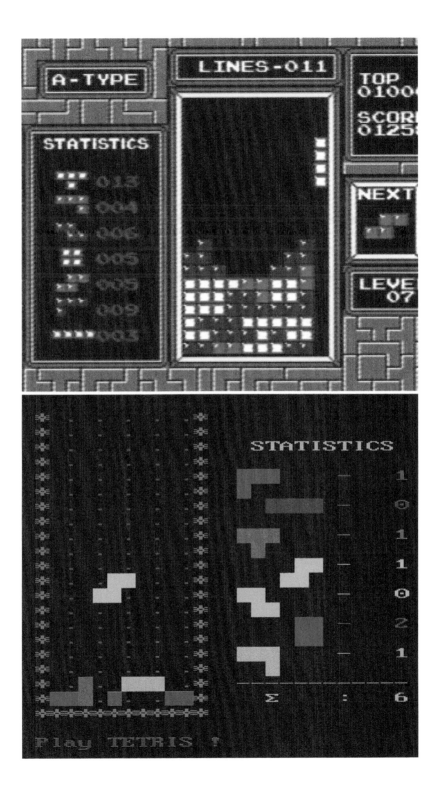

Brothers:
A Tale of Two Sons

X360, XONE, PS3, PS4, PC   First Released **Aug 7, 2013**

In Brothers: A Tale of Two Sons, you must undertake a journey to heal your ailing father by retrieving a curative draught from the distant mountains. You set out from your humble seaside village, pass through bountiful farmlands, and head up into the rocky hills. The vibrant, idyllic scenery evokes a classic storybook adventure, and indeed, Brothers often feels like a fairytale. A young hero sets out to save a loved one against difficult odds, finding danger and companionship along the way. That's nice and all, but haven't we heard this one before?

The thing that sets Brothers apart is right there in the title; there isn't one hero of this tale, there are two. As the player, you must use a controller to play as both brothers simultaneously; your left hand takes control of the responsible elder brother, while your right takes on the playful younger brother. It's disorienting at first to split your attention between two different characters as you clumsily try to move them in tandem, but you soon get the hang of it, and Brothers begins to work its magic.

Each brother has their own way of talking to the people they encounter, and each has their own skills to use in solving the environmental puzzles. The siblings must work together just as your left and right hands work together, and your physical connection to them through the controller feels like the bond that completes the circle of this virtual brotherhood. It's a powerful and intimate sensation, one that Brothers tests the limits of as the journey progresses. By the time you finish this tale, you'll have experienced a remarkable achievement in interactive storytelling, and a testament to the emotional power of this medium.

Animal Crossing:
New Leaf

3DS   First Released **November 8, 2012**

This is a game about doing chores. This is a game about renovating your home. This is a game about paying off your mortgage. This is a game about funding civic improvements. This is a game about catching bugs. Animal Crossing: New Leaf is a game about a litany of tasks that don't sound like all that much fun, and aren't actually all that much fun to do. So why would it make the bucket list?

Because checking off a list of chores is satisfying. Because purchasing that special rug can really tie a room together. Because paying off a debt brings a swell of relief. Because making the town look better makes everyone feel better. Because looking at bugs in the museum is cool. Animal Crossing: New Leaf is a game about the power of small pleasures and the surprisingly positive effect they can have on your life.

In your role as the human mayor of a town populated with animal people, you don't really have many responsibilities. You can get involved with town policy and work to improve your surroundings, or you can go fishing every day and buy yourself new shoes with the proceeds. You can visit towns created by other players, or you can stick to socializing with your own quirky neighbors. There is an abundant variety of things to do, and you're free to be as dedicated or lackadaisical as you want. Within the world of Animal Crossing, there is no wrong way to play and the dramas are fodder for gossip, not grand adventures.

You don't step up to the challenge of Animal Crossing, you surrender to satisfaction of it. Once you give yourself over to the cozy rhythms of your cute little town, New Leaf cultivates a sense of serenity and control that is remarkably soothing. And couldn't we all use a little more of that in our lives?

XCOM: Enemy Unknown

PC, PS3, X360, MAC, iOS, AND   First Released **Oct 8, 2012**

Do you like being stressed out? Do you enjoy agonizing over every decision you make? Do you feel comfortable taking people's lives into your own hands? If so, then XCOM: Enemy Unknown may be the game for you. If you relish the sweet relief that comes from a hard-fought victory, if you want the satisfaction of seeing your leadership bear fruit, and if you know that high stakes make for the highest rewards, then XCOM: Enemy Unknown is definitely the game for you.

As the leader of the XCOM project, you are responsible for saving humanity from a massive alien invasion. Your responsibilities are twofold: guide the research and development of the XCOM base, and command your troops in field against your dangerous enemies. Fortifying your base requires you to select research programs, oversee troop development, manage global crisis zones, and allocate your budget wisely. It doesn't sound terribly dramatic, but managing this economy is an engaging strategic challenge, and once you see how it affects your combat effectiveness, it takes on a whole new gravity.

You only deploy a handful of soldiers per mission, and their movement and combat tactics are totally under your control. But these aren't nameless grunts; they are specialized units that you upgrade and outfit to suit your combat needs, and you quickly grow attached to them. Meticulously taking apart an alien squad is brutally satisfying thanks to the excellent combat system, but one wrong move can result in absolute disaster. When a soldier dies on the field, they can't be revived. Losing your ace sniper, Queen Frostine (yes, you can name them), because you tried to claim an elevated position without properly scouting is heartbreaking. This threat of personal loss compounds the tension on the global scale, making each squad decision and each budgetary line item feel immensely important. The drama may be virtual, but the emotional highs and lows of XCOM: Enemy Unknown are all too real.

IN MEMORIAM

Rest in Peace, Queen Frostine. May your soul float forever on the Ice Cream Sea.

Forza Motorsport 5

XONE   First Released **Nov 22, 2013**

What do you think when you see a car? Do you see a fascinating mechanical marvel full of intriguing, complex systems that you want to understand? Does it stoke an envious desire if it happens to be better than whatever you're driving at the time? Or is it just that box-on-wheels in your driveway that you like to go fast in from time to time? No matter where you are on the spectrum of automotive appreciation, Forza Motorsport 5 has a car for you.

From sleek hypercars that look like they belong in on a magazine cover to zippy hatchbacks that look like they belong in a grocery store parking lot, there is a great variety of vehicles to choose from and you can start your career with any class of car you like. Your guides are trio of hosts from the British TV show, Top Gear, and their knowledge and charisma are a delight even if you don't know an Acura from an Alfa Romeo. Further laying out the welcome mat are the spectacular visuals; the cars are rendering in dazzling detail and the tracks you drive them on are lovely to behold.

But you're not there for a scenic tour (for that vibe, see Forza Horizon 2); you're here to race. With numerous driving assists and an oops-didn't-mean-it rewind function, you can get competitive even if you don't consider yourself competitive. But if you do, start scaling back those assists, delve into the extensive tuning and customization options, and test your skills against the crafty artificial intelligence that is among the best in the racing biz. Forza Motorsport 5 takes its racing very seriously, but it isn't oppressively serious about it. This is a game that wants you to love cars as much as it loves cars, and after taking a few laps with it, you just might.

Rocket League

First Released **Jul 7, 2015**

There are a lot of great video games about sports. Some are realistic simulations, capturing the look and feel of a professional broadcast impeccably (like NBA 2K15 and FIFA 15). Others are arcade reimaginings, taking the familiar and infusing it with some over-the-top fun (like NBA Jam and Mario Strikers Charged). But one of the games that does the best job of recreating what it feels like to play an actual sport is Rocket League, a game in which you drive a car with a rocket booster on the back. Yes, really.

In Rocket League, two small teams face off in an enclosed arena with a goal at either end. You're essentially playing soccer with a rocket car, and the team dynamics translate perfectly. Defending the goal, intercepting the ball, passing it off of walls, and striking it home all require that you and your teammates work together. Sure, you can score some lucky shots, but that will only get you so far against an organized squad. Being a part of such a squad is immensely satisfying.

And so is ramming your car into a big ball at high speeds and sending it flying through the air! Well, you might start off ramming, but soon you'll realize that sometimes a soft touch is necessary, and your head-on tactics will broaden to include calculated glancing blows, clever backflip passes, and high-flying aerial hits. You have sublime control over your vehicle, and this is where Rocket League shows its genius. The abstraction of pressing a button to throw or kick is gone; you are controlling the "kick" and your car-maneuvering skills have a direct, tactile connection to the flight of the ball. This creates an incredible feeling of immediacy and control, and when you make that perfect strike to arc the ball over your opponent and into the goal? You celebrate all the more exuberantly because you know it was your skills that made it happen.

The Elder Scrolls V:
Skyrim

X360, PS3, PC

First Released **Nov 11, 2011**

The idea of walking down your doorstep and out into the world in search of adventure is a romantic one, but whatever environs you live in, they are unlikely to hide glittering treasure or reveal powerful secrets. They are also unlikely to have giant crabs, giant dragons, and actual giants, but the province of Skyrim has all of these things, and much, much more. This massive open world is abundantly populated with intrigue and opportunity, making it one of the best places to go to feel like an adventurer.

And in Skyrim, the course of your adventure is yours to determine. You may follow the main quest to discover how your destiny is intertwined with the powerful dragons of the realm, or you may choose to champion a faction in the ongoing civil war. You might set out for the mages' college, join the thieves' guild, or curry favor with one of the many orc tribes. Or you could leave missions and organizations and structure behind and simply strike out into the wilds, exploring mountains, plains, forests, caverns, and any number of mysterious ruins simply for the sake of adventure.

Freedom is a heady feeling, especially when there's as much to do with it as there is in Skyrim. Of course, you'd better be handy with the steel, quick with a spell, and ready to flee from danger if you want to last long. Fighting is a part of Skyrim, but so is talking, bartering, deciphering, plotting, crafting, stealing, and too many other "-ings" to list here. Skyrim's staggering diversity makes it one of those marvelous games that stands ready to accommodate any mood. Motivated or aimless, aggressive or agreeable, daring or demure, no matter how you're feeling that day, Skyrim is waiting to welcome you into its incredible world and let you find your place in it.

Sid Meier's Civilization V:
The Complete Edition

PC, MAC   First Released **February 5, 2014**

The title is a bit of a mouthful, but what do you expect from a game in which your goal is to build an empire to stand the test of time? The Civilization series contains some of the grandest strategy games in history, and this one is the reigning champ. The Complete Edition contains some important innovations and additions to the core game, but it's this complex core that makes Civilization V something special.

You start at the beginning of human civilization, ready to found your tribe's first city. Will you start the Incan empire as Pachacuti or get a head start on the England's reign as Elizabeth? Though it is rich with historical information, Civilization V is, after all, a game; don't be surprised if you see Gandhi's bombers facing off against Babylonian tanks. Part of the fun of Civ is learning new things about the world you live in, and part of it is remaking a new world as you see fit.

Victory can come through military dominance, diplomatic influence, scientific prowess, or cultural achievement, and success is the result of thousands of individual decisions. How you develop your cities, where you expand your borders, what technology you research, how you manage your economy, what units you build, and how you deal with other leaders are just some of the myriad strategic challenges you must face over your centuries of rule. You can tweak the options for longer or shorter games, but make no mistake, this is a timely undertaking. Get comfortable, stay hydrated, and prepare to be completely engrossed by the game that has kept millions up into the wee hours of the night saying, "Just one more turn."

TO THE STARS
If discovering alien life and researching futuristic technology is more your speed, Civilization: Beyond Earth brings the complexity of Civ to the final frontier.

Mario Kart 8

WiiU   First Released **May 30, 2014**

Since its debut on the Super Nintendo, the Mario Kart series has been a pillar of Nintendo's pantheon. If you've owned a Nintendo system or knew someone who did, odds are you've dropped some peels or popped some 'shrooms yourself. For those readers concerned about the use of drug slang in the previous sentence, rest assured that those are very literal things you can do in the course of a normal race.

You see, Mario Kart is about racing, and more than many other entries in the series, Mario Kart 8 requires that you take corners well and grab every strategically placed boost opportunity you can in order to stay ahead of the pack. But Mario Kart is also about items; the aforementioned banana peels can cause opponents to spin out at inopportune (and hilarious) times, and the mushrooms can give you a speed burst to help you beat everyone to the line. Firing kart-seeking turtle shells, zapping everyone with a lightning bolt, or hitching your car to a chomp-happy piranha plant aren't just good tactics, they're a whole lot of goofy fun.

And that's what makes Mario Kart such a great game. This is an intensely competitive racing game featuring princesses, a dinosaur, a gorilla, and some babies. The tracks are expertly designed courses that take you into the clouds, under the sea, and up to a rainbow-hued space station. Mario Kart 8 is a beautiful blend of serious and silly that brings people of all ages together to cheer each other on, talk smack to each other, and generally have a grand old time.

TOUR THE CIRCUIT

You can have a blast with Mario Kart on pretty much any Nintendo system, notably with the stellar track selection of the Nintendo DS and the two-seater karts on the GameCube.

LOADING...

31 - 40

Trials Evolution

X360, PC   First Released **Apr 18, 2012**

In Trials Evolution, you ride a motorcycle and try to get the fastest time on each level, so it's a racing game. But the level design has more in common with Mario than MotoGP, so maybe it's a platforming game. And some levels are so tricky that it's difficult to simply figure out how you're going to maneuver through them, so really it's more of a... puzzle game? It may be tough to pin down the exact genre of Trials Evolution, but getting sucked in to overcoming obstacles and shaving seconds off your times is all too easy.

Trials Evolution is about getting to the finish line first, though most of the time you're racing against the clock and not another rider. Viewing your motorcycle through the traditional side-scrolling platformer perspective, you drive up and down ramps, zoom through loop-the-loops, and motor over all kinds of structures. Some courses take place in plausible venues, like industrial spaces or rolling hillsides, while others get more fantastical and take you across canyons, through castles, and up into the clouds. These creative spaces give the game a playful tone that serves to lighten the mood when things get tough.

The levels start out quite easy and focus on speed. By shifting your rider's weight forward and back and managing the throttle, you strive to find the racing line that lets you maintain as much momentum as possible. Later, the focus shifts, and now the challenge becomes figuring out how to get your bike up preposterously steep walls and across yawning chasms. "It looks impossible!" you'll cry, and your rider with flail like a ragdoll with dozens upon dozens of crashes. But then something clicks; you figure out what you need to do and a few tries later, you do it. The rush of satisfaction is powerful, but not as strong as your reignited urge to do it one more time, to do it even faster, and to take on the next trial.

Halo:
Combat Evolved Anniversary

X360, XONE   First Released **Nov 15, 2011**

It may seem strange to say this about the lone representative from one of the most popular and influential first-person shooter franchises, but this bucket list entry comes with a caveat. Play Halo: Combat Evolved Anniversary, but play it with a partner. Whether he is online with voice chat or she is right next to you on the couch, this player will be key to your enjoyment of this enduring classic.

Kicking off with a desperate crash-landing on a mysterious, artificial ring world, things get moving quickly in Halo: CEA. The transition from cramped interiors of your doomed ship to the soaring heights of the halo structure set a sweeping tone for your adventure, and the excellent music score is more than happy to enhance it. This Anniversary version affords the novel ability to switch between Halo: CE's original graphics from 2001 and the revamped visuals created for this 2011 release. Seeing the difference a decade makes with the press of a button is fascinating and revealing, not just of how far technology has advanced, but also of how well the original visual design holds up.

Halo: Combat Evolved introduces Master Chief, an armored supersoldier leading humanity in a losing battle against a coalition of hostile alien races. Though you'll see the same enemies frequently, you won't always see the same tactics as your foes work together in deadly harmony to make combat as tough as you can handle. The deftly balanced trio of guns, grenades, and melee attacks form the basis of your tactics, and when you throw vehicles in the mix, the battlefield becomes a playground of possibilities. And this is why you should play it with a partner, because while this playground can be really fun on your own, it's an absolute blast when you have someone to play with. Rarely is video game combat as collaborative, challenging, and downright fun as it is in a cooperative game of Halo.

Katamari Damacy

PS2, PS3   First Released **Mar 18, 2004**

Though "play" is the most common verb associated with video games, there aren't all that many games that actually feel like "play" as we first learn it in childhood. The spontaneity and creativity of a child's play often seems like something we reserve for our younger years, but when you play games like Katamari Damacy, it all comes rushing back.

Your mission is an absurd one. Your father, the King of All Cosmos, has accidentally destroyed all of the stars and the moon (whoops!), and it's up to you, little prince, to repopulate the heavens by rolling a very sticky ball around on Earth and gathering up enough material to make stars.

You have to start small, of course, so you cruise around a home office, picking up thumb tacks, paper clips, ants, and such. As your ball gets bigger, you can roll up bigger things, so pretty soon you're adding books, computers, desk chairs, and people to your big ball of stuff. Venturing outside, you get bushes, benches, trees, and cows in on the action, and before too long, houses, office buildings, and mountains. The reactions of the creatures you capture are cute, and the cheery soundtrack is the perfect accompaniment to your pursuit.

It's all so totally bizarre, and so totally delightful. Tackling an elaborate task born out of a silly premise feels like making your own fun, and in many ways, that's what Katamari Damacy is: fun for the sake of fun. It's boisterous and rejuvenative and joyful and so unlike anything you'll do in your daily life that you owe it to yourself to make time for Katamari Damacy, to make time for play.

Grand Theft Auto V

PS3, PS4, X360, XONE, PC   First Released **Sep 17, 2013**

The most notorious name in video games earned its reputation for a reason. Not only are most of the people in the Grand Theft Auto series cynical caricatures, but the games also give you astonishing liberty to beat, stab, shoot, run over, blow up, and kill almost anyone you meet. Whether you're firing on cops after you knock over a jewelry store or battering a pedestrian with a golf club because he insulted your haircut, the opportunities for mayhem are seemingly endless. Grand Theft Auto V is not a game for young, impressionable minds.

It is a game for criminal masterminds who want to plan and execute daring heists. It is a game for vehicle enthusiasts who want to race around a virtual Los Angeles in a sports car, tear through the wilderness on a dirt bike, or fly under bridges in an airplane. It is a game for fashionistas, movie-goers, golfers, swimmers, real estate moguls, base jumpers, mountain bikers, truckers, boaters, and sky divers. And yes, it is a game for mayhem seekers who want to laugh while the world burns.

Grand Theft Auto V set you up on some incredible missions in the course of its story, and there are three protagonists that you can switch between at almost any time. Not only does this fuel some excellent dramatic moments, but the three personalities encourage you to play in different ways. Even if you generally try to do right by the virtual people you meet, playing as the brilliantly maniacal Trevor frees you to indulge your chaotic impulses. And this freedom is the greatest gift GTA V bestows. It is a world full of action figures for you to play with in any way you see fit, a virtual sandbox without equal that earned its reputation as one of the most beloved names in video games for a reason.

Super Metroid

SNES, WII, WiiU   First Released **Mar 19, 1994**

The march of time is not kind to every video game. Many games that introduced new innovations, set new standards, and captured the adoration of gamers around the world have lost their luster as the years go on. Time has a way of retiring games, relegating them to be remembered for the games they inspired rather than inspiring people to play them. Some games, however, shine on undiminished, and while infinite are the arguments of fanboys, there is one thing most people agree on: Super Metroid is still awesome.

In the eerie caverns of the planet Zebes, an entity of great power waits in the wrong hands. As the intrepid bounty hunter Samus Aran, it's up to you to brave the dangers within and avert disaster. Even decades after its release, Super Metroid is a wonderfully atmospheric adventure. The music is a masterwork of grim foreboding laced with heroic strains, and the dank caves and alien foes look as perilous as ever. Technical standards may change constantly, but artistic excellence endures.

The same can be said for brilliant design. Though the complex you explore is large, you can't just blast your way wherever you want to go. Instead, you gain access to new areas by acquiring new abilities and weapons that not only act as keys to the kingdom, but also fundamentally change the way you move and the way you fight. This marriage of map exploration and player evolution sucks you in and spurs you onward, making you eager to see what's around the next corner and to find out what trick you'll learn next. It's an immensely gratifying system, one that has been imitated and duplicated to great effect in many other games. But these heirs to throne haven't unseated Super Metroid, they have only paid homage to it. Hail to the queen, baby.

METROIDVANIA

Noun. Term used to describe games that adhere to designs popularized by the Metroid and Castlevania series. Standout examples include Shadow Complex and Axiom Verge.

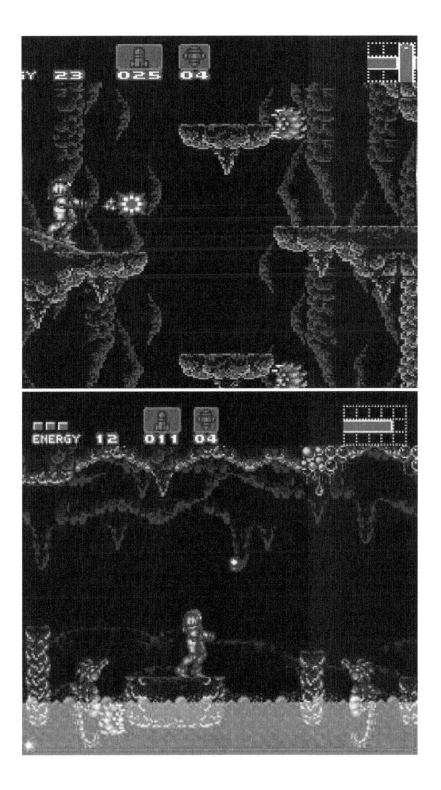

Her Story

PC, iOS, MAC   First Released **Jun 23, 2015**

Video games are an interactive medium. This interaction often requires that you learn about a variety of systems, develop your skills to accomplish things more efficiently, and exert your influence on the outcome of the experience. But what if the outcome seemed like a foregone conclusion? What if the only skill you needed was the ability to use a search engine? What if you weren't learning about systems, but about people? Though Her Story may not fit the mold many have cast for video games, it's an utterly engrossing experience in which you have a very unique part to play.

Simon Smith is dead, and it's up to you to find out who killed him. But this isn't a police procedural in which you visit crime scenes, chase down perps, and bite off more than you can chew. Instead, you sit at a computer that looks about two decades old and search through video files of seven interviews that the police conducted with Hannah Smith, Simon's widow. These are actual videos, mind you, and Hannah is played by an actual actress, not a computer-generated character.

But you can only call up short clips of the interviews, and you can only find a clip by searching for a word that Hannah speaks in it. This piecemeal approach means that you're constantly listening for words that might lead you to a new clip, or thinking of related terms as you slowly piece the story together. The heady thrill of discovering a fruitful lead, the creeping frustration of chasing dead ends, and the burning curiosity to find the truth are all brilliantly realized here. Her Story brings to life the intrigue and uncertainty of investigation as only an interactive medium can and embodies one of the best things about the video game industry. Year after year, the mold is broken anew, bringing us fascinating new experiences and new ways to play.

Kerbal Space Program

PC, MAC   First Released **June 24, 2011**

Kerbal Space Program is a game about little green people and space. Rather than blasting them out of the sky as many video games would have you do, KSP wants you to blast them into the sky. And you won't be shooting them into the stratosphere with circus cannons, giant slingshots, or any other goofy contraption that would seem a natural fit for their googly eyes and toothy smiles. You'll be meticulously designing elaborate spacecraft to break the shackles of earthly gravity, reach orbit, and explore the solar system. This is a rigorous simulation in which you become the brains behind a very serious space program for very silly little humanoids.

Though you can jump right in to the design workshop and start bolting together any spaceship you can come up with, it's best to choose the mode that eases you in by slowly unlocking new spaceship parts as you complete missions designed to teach you the many facets of KSP. And there are many, many facets to learn. The extensive physics simulation calculates how every single object on your ship will affect its trajectory, and it soon becomes clear that the complexity of building a ship that will fly is impressive. To land on another planet? Astounding.

But that's getting ahead of yourself. Start by building a plane that can go really fast and not explode. Then aim for the upper atmosphere, put a satellite in orbit, and set your sights on the next challenge. Dozens and dozens of crashes, explosions, and other failures await, but stick with it, you're going places. And when you do, you won't just feel excited and happy and relieved; you'll feel proud. You'll feel smart. You'll feel like you've accomplished something significant, because you have. There's a reason that NASA has taken an interest in Kerbal Space Program. It's rocket science brought to life in a video game, and it's brilliant.

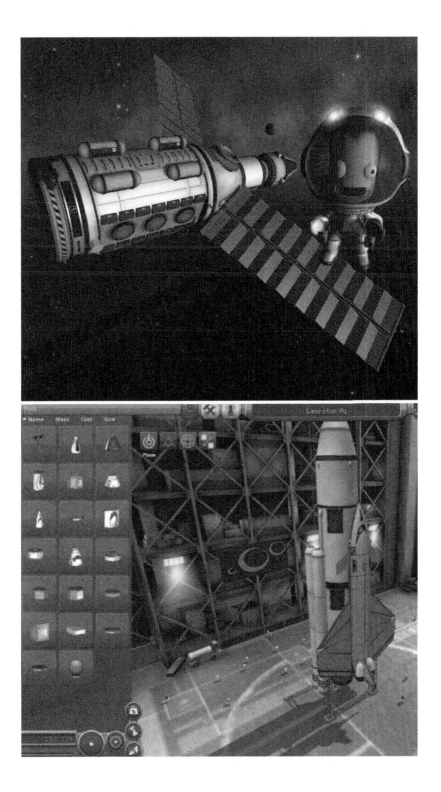

The Secret of Monkey Island:
Special Edition

X360, PC, PS3, MAC   First Released **Jul 15, 2009**

Of all the heroes that video games have given us over the years, Guybrush Threepwood may be one of the least likely. He's not particularly strong or quick, he has no noble aspirations, and what's up with that name? Yes, Guybrush Threepwood is an odd duck, but this makes him perfectly suited to be the protagonist of this unusually clever and uncommonly funny point-and-click adventure game.

The secret of Monkey Island is what Guybrush is after, and he's hoping it's a heaping pile of treasure. But to become the pirate he needs to be, he must contend with all sorts of savory (the beautiful governor) and unsavory (the evil ghost pirate) characters. Playing this Special Edition gives you the added benefit of being able to switch between the original graphics from 1990 and the lively visuals from 2009. The original art still conveys a rich sense of character and packs in delightful details, so you may be tempted to stick with it even though the new version's voice actors are an appealing bunch.

Whether you're listening to the dialogue or reading it, prepare to be entertained. A brilliant sense of humor suffuses the entire game, from the conversations you have with the colorful locals to the quests you must undertake. Be it buying transportation from a smarmy used ship salesman or slinging insults at a sword fight, solving the puzzles the game sets before you is a brainy delight (and there's even a hint system if you need a little nudge). The Secret of Monkey Island: Special Edition paints a wonderfully wacky picture of the pirate's life, one in which a rubber chicken with a pulley in the middle can be an item of great importance, and a goofball named Guybrush Threepwood can become a hero adored by all.

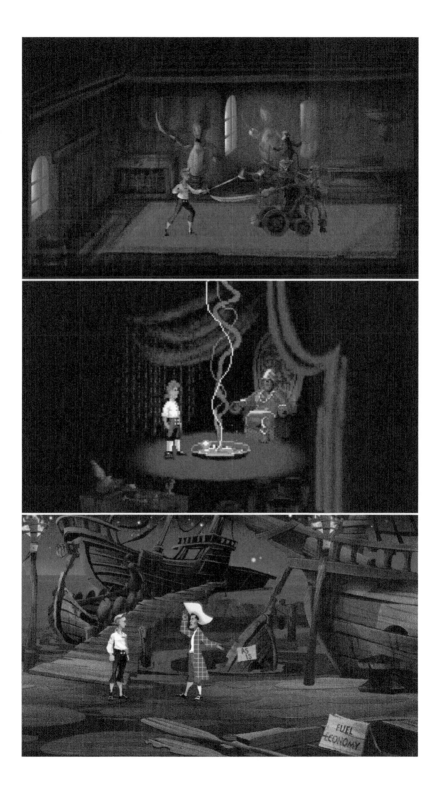

Surgeon Simulator 2013

PC, MAC, iOS, PS4, AND   First Released **Apr 19, 2013**

Surgery is a delicate endeavor, fraught with danger and only advisable for highly trained specialists who have years and years of experience. To imitate such an action in a video game would require complex systems modeling human anatomy and finely tuned controls that allowed for the utmost in player precision. Extensive simulations have been designed with exactly this level of engineering, but Surgeon Simulator is not one of them.

Instead, it is the opposite. As you move your surgeon's hand above the sedated patient, it swoops back and forth with a momentum that is difficult to control. Reaching for your instrument, you are as likely to grab a clock radio as a scalpel thanks to the odd finger controls (and what is a clock radio even doing there, anyway?). Finally lining up your incision, you delicately move in only to stab the patient in the armpit. Or the neck. Or the eye. You are the worst surgeon ever, and it's absolutely hilarious.

For all the time we spend trying to avoid clumsiness in our lives, it is liberating to play a game in which clumsiness is the whole point. The patients in Surgeon Simulator are resilient (and sedated, thankfully), but you'll still cringe as you crack ribs willy-nilly and then root around in the chest cavity for a sickly lung. Don't worry, the cartoon visuals will keep your squeamishness at bay, and odds are you'll be too busy laughing uproariously at how hard it is to perform basic actions to notice how quickly your patient is dying (or that you dropped your watch inside him). The utter absurdity of Surgeon Simulator makes it an absolute joy to play, or to watch someone play, or even to think about after you've played it. It's the goofy, gratuitous gift that keeps on giving.

SILLIER AND SILLIER

For more gleeful absurdity, flop around a kitchen as a slice of bread in I Am Bread (by this same developer), or suit up as an octopus secretly trying to be a normal suburban dad in Octodad: Dadliest Catch.

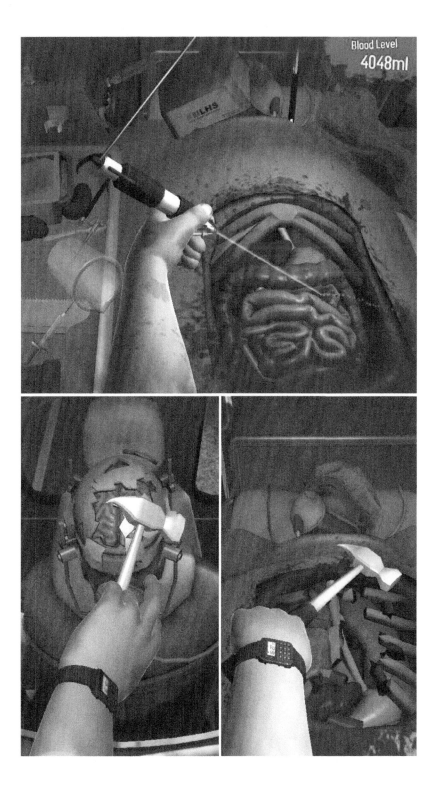

Dark Souls

PS3, X360, PC   First Released **Sep 22, 2011**

Whoever told you it was great to be a knight in shining armor has never played Dark Souls. It. Is. Terrifying. There are legions of nefarious creatures out to kill you in this third-person action game, from chambling undead soldiers and vicious giant rats to towering gargoyles and fearsome dragons. And though there's no storybook charm to be found here, the menacing menagerie you face is so fantastically designed that your desire to see what new fiend awaits you will be as powerful as your desire to run away from it.

Run, or don't; it doesn't really matter. Death with find you in Dark Souls, but it is only through adversity (i.e. dying a lot) that you will grow stronger. Every enemy is a threat to you, which means every fight matters, and this immediacy is invigorating. As you dodge and block and slash with your medieval weapons, you learn to watch your enemies' movement, to match them in deadly combat, and eventually, to defeat them. Success in Dark Souls is success hard-earned, and few games can deliver sweeter satisfaction.

You will have your triumphant moments and abject defeats, but one pleasure that Dark Souls consistently delivers is the joy of exploration. This is one of the most ingeniously crafted worlds in all of gaming, one in which towering castles, filthy alleys, dense forests, deep caverns, and dozens of other beautifully realized areas are all linked together. Slowly figuring out how it all connects is so rewarding that simply opening a locked door is a moment to treasure. Of course, nothing is simple in Dark Souls, but that's what makes it so special. Dark Souls makes you earn it, but when you do earn it, even a little bit, it's empowering in a way you never thought a video game could be.

LOADING...

41 - 50

The Sims 3

PC, MAC, PS3, X360, Wii, DS, 3DS, Mobile   First Released **Jun 2, 2009**

What would you do if you had complete control over everyone in your neighborhood? Would you cheer up Linda from down the street by sending her to the library and then buying her a new chair to read in? Maybe you would help Andy, the businessman, spend a little more time with his true passion, painting. Or perhaps you'd bestow tricks instead of treats, sending Pam to kiss another man in front of her husband, or putting curtains dangerously close to Jerry's oven. In The Sims 3, all of these manipulations are possible, as are so, so many more.

The Sims 3 is game about life; specifically, the lives of some virtual people that you design. Do you replicate your friends and family to meddle with their fates or do you imagine entirely new people? It's up to you. Once created, you plunk them down in a house and start managing their lives. Where do they spend their time, what do they do, and who do they do it with? There is no right or wrong answer to any of these questions; you have complete freedom to do as you will.

The beauty of The Sims 3 lies in the variety of things you can do with this freedom. Adult sims have professions, but they also have free time in which to go to the gym, play guitar, and tend a garden, or neglect their loved ones, shout at the neighbors, and quit their jobs. You can renovate the house to better host parties, or you can board up the bathroom so no one can ever pee. Whether you are a benevolent or mischievous overlord, the Sims prove to be a lively, entertaining, and endearing breed of virtual folk. The Sims 3 brings them to life in an intriguingly complex world, and losing yourself in the triumphs and trials of their virtual lives is a truly enjoyable way to spend hours and hours of your actual one.

Persona 4 Golden

VITA   First Released **Jun 14, 2012**

High school can be a tough time, especially if you've just moved to a new city. You have to make new friends, get involved in activities, keep up with your own studies, and work out how to fit it all in to your busy schedule. And then there are the monsters you have to fight at night in a supernatural television world in order to prevent a real-world serial killer from claiming more victims. No wonder teens are so stressed these days!

All of these challenges await you in Persona 4 Golden, an enhanced remake of the excellent Shin Megami Tensei: Persona 4. Yes, even managing your daily schedule. This is a role-playing game in which much of your role is to be a high school student. Choosing to study or join a club can pay off in your nightly battles, but the most rewarding daytime activities are the ones you spend with your friends. The characters in P4G are lively, nuanced, and charismatic, thanks to stellar writing and great voice acting. As you get to know them, your relationships deepen and you find yourself eager for the next time you get to talk them. They confide in you about their worries and hopes, and prompt you to think about your own life in the way that a good friend might. As virtual relationships go, the ones in P4G are some of the absolute best.

Once night falls, however, the stresses of high school fall away and the trials of combat begin. Fighting as a team, you and your friends must use your complementary abilities to not only vanquish enemies in the mysterious TV world, but also to find out what the heck is going on. The combat system is deep and engaging, and its connection to your daytime activities make it all the more satisfying. Persona 4 Golden is a lengthy, engrossing adventure, one that will (however improbably) make you excited for each new school day.

Batman:
Arkham Asylum

X360, PS3, PC, MAC   First Released **Aug 25, 2009**

One of the greatest gifts a video game can bestow is the opportunity to inhabit a character. Games have given us some great original characters, but who wouldn't want to play as their favorite heroes and villains from movies, TV shows, and comics? Alas, the history of licensed characters in video games is littered with disappointing efforts that fail to capture the appeal of the legends we love. There are some good licensed games, however, even some great ones. And then there's Batman: Arkham Asylum, an outstanding adventure that does such a superb job of letting you be the bat that it ranks among Batman's best appearances in any form of media.

So what is it like to be the hero Gotham deserves? In Arkham Asylum, Batman is powerful; you take on packs of criminals and subdue them with rhythmic beatdowns that look stylish and pack a satisfying punch. Batman is stealthy; you sneak through areas and pick off enemies, lying in wait to grab them as they patrol by or using your cape to swoop in from above like a bird of prey. Batman is crafty; your arsenal of gadgets includes a grapnel hook for evasive maneuvers, explosive gel for setting booby traps, and batarangs for striking anything and anyone you see fit. Put it all together and you've got a brilliant recipe for living the Batman dream.

Of course, Batman wouldn't be Batman without sinister villains, and with the Joker arriving at the infamous Arkham Asylum, it's not long until all hell breaks loose. Your encounters with the Scarecrow, Harley Quinn, and other classic adversaries are wonderfully dramatic, and solving the hundreds of puzzles posed by The Riddler is an obsession-worthy challenge. It's a thrill for fans of the cape and cowl, but Arkham Asylum isn't just an excellent Batman game. It's an excellent game, period.

The Walking Dead

PC, MAC, X360, XONE, PS3, PS4, VITA, iOS, AND   First Released **Aug 24, 2012**

Zombies: can't live with 'em, can't find a shelf in a video game store without 'em. It's easy to see why these dehumanized former humans are so popular as antagonists, but for all the great and not-so-great games dedicated to destroying the undead, those brain-hungry monsters aren't actually that interesting. It's the situations people get forced into by zombies that lead to really intriguing stories, and no game knows this better than The Walking Dead.

Though it is based in the world of the superb comics by the same name, this episodic series by developer Telltale Games focuses on characters and stories that are unique to the game. You play as Lee, an escaped convict who meets up with a young girl named Clementine in the early days of the zombie outbreak. With Clem's parents nowhere to be found, you take charge of her safety, and thus begins one of the most memorable relationships in all of gaming. Most of what you do in The Walking Dead is talk, and the words you choose and the decisions you make determine much about how Lee and Clem get along in their efforts to survive.

But it's not just you two out there. In the face of a terrifying and ubiquitous threat, you team up with a cast of characters that run a relatable gamut of personality. Your choices mold your relationships with others, which in turn affect the course of the game in different ways. Some consequences you see immediately, while others develop over the course of your struggle. You will hold the fate of someone you care about in your hands more than once, and you won't be able to save everyone. Far from the usual zombie-slaying power fantasy, The Walking Dead forces you to look at how powerless you can really be. It is a grim, often gut-wrenching game that spans five episodes, and seeing it through to the end is a powerfully affecting journey.

THEN WHAT?

After the first five episodes conclude, the story continues and if you play Season 2 on the same system as you played Season 1, you can import your save files and continue your personal story.

The Legend of Zelda:
Ocarina of Time 3D

3DS   First Released **Jun 16, 2011**

As one of the best games in one of the most successful series in video game history, The Legend of Zelda: Ocarina of Time is one of the most common answers you'll hear to the question, "What is the greatest game of all time?" But this book isn't here to open that can of worms, it's just here to get you to play this fantastic game.

It starts as many legends do, with a young boy finding that he is destined for something different, and then setting off into the world to find his fate. Leaving the cozy, verdant embrace of your home in Kokiri Forest and heading out into unknown wilds of Hyrule Field feels like the start of something grand, as indeed it is. Your travels take you to towering castles and bustling villages, dangerous caverns and mysterious deserts. Along the way, you encounter a diverse cast of characters, some of whom become dear friends by the time your journey ends. You also run afoul of all kinds of feisty enemies whom you must dispatch using an arsenal that's as emblematic of the series as your green tunic and cap.

Hyrule is a beautiful, lively place, brimming with visual flourishes and vibrant details added for this thoroughly improved version for the Nintendo 3DS. But the element that has always elevated Ocarina to such lofty heights is its music. The places you go and the people you meet are accompanied by distinctive melodies that deepen your connection to them, and the songs you play on your ocarina will echo in your memories long after your adventure is complete. Ocarina of Time uses the power of music to create a wonderfully memorable adventure, one you'll be happy to reminisce about each time one of its tunes pops into your head.

HEY! LISTEN!

The 3DS not only got another revamped N64 Zelda classic in Majora's Mask, it features one of the best Zelda games, Link Between Worlds, and can play the two Nintendo DS Zelda games. That's a lotta Link!

Geometry Wars:
Retro Evolved 2

X360   First Released **Jul 30, 2008**

There was a time when arcades were king, and in this time, there was no room for slow-burn gameplay, complex systems, or sweeping narratives. It was a time of instant action, of clear directives, and of swiftly escalating challenges. While some games seemed to glow with a greed for quarters, others were incandescent with tantalizing cleverness and electrifying intensity. The titans of that era still inspire designers today, and one of the best modern torchbearers of this legacy is Geometry Wars: Retro Evolved 2.

Geometry Wars is a game about moving your neon shape around a confined 2D space and blasting other neon shapes before they blast you. At first, your movements are methodical and confident as you cut a swath through the opposition; as your foes multiply, you must become swifter and more agile. Weaving past enemies and dodging projectiles as you frantically blast a clear path through the increasing chaos is a dance with neon death that you almost always lose. But look at your score, was it a little higher this time? Did you last a little longer? Honing your skills and then seeing the results reflected in bigger and bigger numbers is a time-honored strain of satisfaction that remains as potent as ever.

The many modes of Retro Evolved 2 test your talents in different ways, and all the while the score-multiplying wreckage of your enemies tempts you to fly ever closer to the proverbial sun. The pinnacle of this temptation is the superlative Pacifism mode, in which you don't fire a shot, but instead skirt danger with bold flight maneuvers that make you feel like a neon daredevil. Okay, yes, there is a lot of neon in this game, but it pops and fizzles with crackling energy against the starlit background, the futuristic dream of an arcade starfighter brought to life brilliantly. The arcade is dead. Long live the arcade.

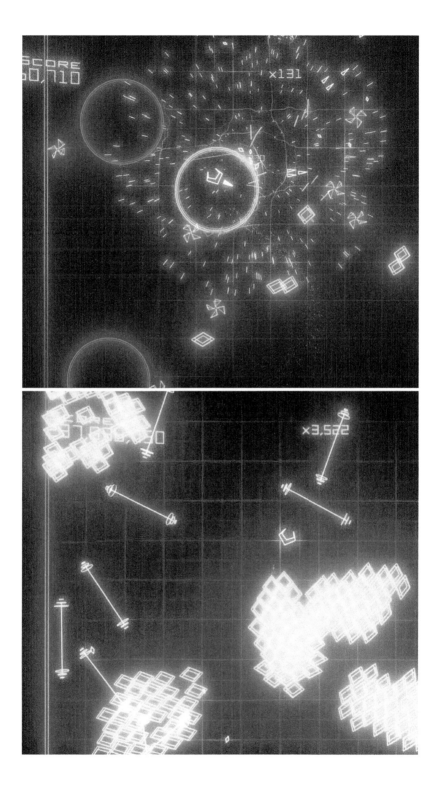

Mega Man 2

NES, PS, Wii, WiiU, 3DS, PS3, PSP, VITA   First Released **Dec 24, 1988**

Mega Man has been around for a long time on the home console timescale, and he ranks among the most prolific video game protagonists. His popularity and longevity are due to a number of factors, but it's fair to say that one of the biggest reasons for his superstar status is Mega Man 2. This is the game that minted the Blue Bomber, and to this day it stands as a testament to how legends are born.

Unlike some video game heroes who rely on performance-enhancing mushrooms and flowers to gird themselves for battle, Mega Man packs a punch right from the get-go. Leaping across perilous pits and blasting foes with his arm cannon, you fight your way to the end of each stage to face a formidable boss. Each of the Robot Masters is a tough adversary that you must outwit and outmaneuver, and though your hard-fought victory is a reward in its own right, you also gain the power of your defeated foe. These abilities aren't simply more powerful ways to kill your enemies, though having the right weapon for the right boss is crucial. They also have unique properties, so the spinning leaf shield of Wood Man has a very different utility than, say, the atomic fire of Heat Man.

Using these utilities in the right situation takes some figuring out, but the real challenge of Mega Man 2 rests squarely on your dexterity. The levels are littered with enemies who make your platforming progress difficult, but the superb soundtrack fuels you onward with tunes so catchy that you'll be glad to have them stuck in your head (and they will get stuck in your head). There's no doubt that Mega Man 2 stands the test of time. The question is, will you stand the test of Mega Man 2?

Super Smash Bros.
for Wii U

WiiU   First Released **Nov 21, 2014**

Two swords clash as legendary heroes meet in battle. Powerful princesses exchange blows, fighting for the honor of their realms. A robot boy with a gun for an arm shoots at a lady in a gun-armed spacesuit. A gorilla throws a barrel at a hedgehog, while a doctor hits a dragon with a baseball bat. A dinosaur swallows a fitness trainer. A pink ball sings another pink ball to sleep.

This may sound like a writer slowly losing his mind, and sometimes the sheer chaos of Super Smash Bros. for Wii U can seem a little unhinged. But there is a method to this madness, and it starts with simplicity. Though this is a fighting game, there are no elaborate button combinations to learn or complex meters to manage. The barrier to entry is low, welcoming anyone with the ability to press a few buttons and the willingness to whack Mario with a mallet. At the same time, the skill ceiling is high, allowing players to dive deep into the subtleties of different moves, items, and strategies to gain an edge in the fierce competition.

The beauty of Super Smash Bros. is that it bridges these two extremes so deftly. The roster of beloved characters from Mario, Zelda, Donkey Kong, Pokémon, and other iconic series makes for some very silly match-ups, and the array of items in play amplifies this tone. No one likes to be pounded into oblivion, but getting walloped by a hammer wielded by a giant, smiling penguin creature is a different story. And how mad can you really get at your sister for outmaneuvering you, when all she wanted to do was eat a tomato? The answer is very mad, actually, but you won't stay that way for long. Super Smash Bros. cultivates competition and camaraderie, making it an excellent way to bring friends together, or to make some new ones.

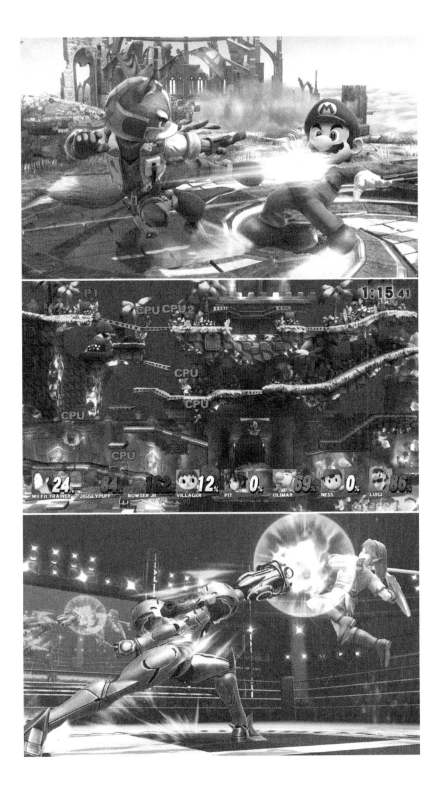

Final Fantasy VI

SNES, PS, GBA, PS3, PSP, VITA, Wii, iOS   First Released **Apr 2, 1994**

Nostalgia is a powerful force in the video game industry. The advance of technology fuels the release of dozens of remasters and remakes every year as players eagerly revisit the games of their past and publishers eagerly sell them. If a franchise grows big enough, the name alone is enough to entice millions of players, and by that measure, few franchises are more enticing than Final Fantasy. This sprawling series could fill a bucket list of its own, but to understand why it has garnered such admiration, you need only play Final Fantasy VI.

Some tales of adventure and heroism star a single hero, but Final Fantasy VI features a bevy of them. They are bound together by their opposition to the evil Empire, but it's up to you to decide how they grow as a fighting force. Whether you develop their innate abilities or use armor, weapons, and other equipment to mold them to different combat roles, the tactical development of your fighters is a gratifying pursuit and combat is an engaging challenge. Though fighting is frequent, there are a variety of other quests and activities (some quite comical) that help mark out a spirited cadence for your journey.

The ensemble cast develops beautifully as you progress, revealing more and more of their stories and making you a part of their lives. And of course, no epic role-playing game is complete without a memorable nemesis. The maniacal Kefka is one of the greatest villains you will find anywhere, a fiend who inspires such utter loathing that every encounter with him is all the more meaningful. The memorable characters draw you into the grand adventure, and the unforgettable soundtrack elevates the whole experience to even greater heights. To play Final Fantasy VI is to plant the seed of your own nostalgia, so play it, and do your future self a favor.

Super Mario Galaxy 2

Wii, Wii U   First Released **May 23, 2010**

The biggest star of the video game world wears blue overalls, white gloves, and a bright red hat. The pinnacle of style, he ain't, but Mario is an icon, and his enduring popularity is largely thanks to the incredible game designers at Nintendo. Over the years and across many genres, they have consistently cast Mario in creative, challenging, and joyful games to the delight of millions around the world. Super Mario Galaxy 2 is one of the greatest of these, an amazing showcase of the ingenuity and passion that has been Nintendo's gift to the world of gaming.

In Super Mario Galaxy, our hero took to the stars in search of stars (well, where else would you go?). Spherical levels of varying sizes gave you the feeling of tromping around on little planets, and the clever layouts made each new level fun to explore. In Super Mario Galaxy 2, new power-ups and design elements are introduced at such a feverish pace that you play the game in a perpetual state of joy and wonder, eager to see what each new level will bring.

On one level you might be ice-skating, and on another, creating clouds to help you cross a yawning divide. You could be riding on Yoshi through a three-dimensional space one moment, then navigating gravitational shifts in a two-dimensional area the next. There are breezy levels and tough challenges in abundance, and they are all presented with colorful, charming visuals and a captivating soundtrack. Super Mario Galaxy 2 doesn't just embody what's great about Mario, it embodies what is great about video games. The beauty of animation and sound, the creativity of design, the satisfaction of overcoming a challenge, and the joy of play are all part of the artistry of game development, and Super Mario Galaxy 2 masterfully exemplifies them all.

My Bucket List

☐ Spelunky	☆ ☆ ☆ ☆ ☆
☐ Assassin's Creed II	☆ ☆ ☆ ☆ ☆
☐ Dead Space	☆ ☆ ☆ ☆ ☆
☐ The Last of Us Remastered	☆ ☆ ☆ ☆ ☆
☐ Portal 2	☆ ☆ ☆ ☆ ☆
☐ Mass Effect 2	☆ ☆ ☆ ☆ ☆
☐ Gone Home	☆ ☆ ☆ ☆ ☆
☐ Journey	☆ ☆ ☆ ☆ ☆
☐ Red Dead Redemption	☆ ☆ ☆ ☆ ☆
☐ Uncharted 2: Among Thieves	☆ ☆ ☆ ☆ ☆
☐ Nidhogg	☆ ☆ ☆ ☆ ☆
☐ Psychonauts	☆ ☆ ☆ ☆ ☆
☐ Superbrothers: Sword & Sworcery EP	☆ ☆ ☆ ☆ ☆
☐ Super Meat Boy	☆ ☆ ☆ ☆ ☆
☐ Rock Band 3	☆ ☆ ☆ ☆ ☆
☐ The Witcher 3: Wild Hunt	☆ ☆ ☆ ☆ ☆
☐ Super Mario World	☆ ☆ ☆ ☆ ☆
☐ Half-Life 2	☆ ☆ ☆ ☆ ☆
☐ God of War III	☆ ☆ ☆ ☆ ☆
☐ StarCraft II: Wings of Liberty	☆ ☆ ☆ ☆ ☆
☐ Minecraft	☆ ☆ ☆ ☆ ☆
☐ Tetris	☆ ☆ ☆ ☆ ☆
☐ Brothers: A Tale of Two Sons	☆ ☆ ☆ ☆ ☆
☐ Animal Crossing: New Leaf	☆ ☆ ☆ ☆ ☆
☐ XCOM: Enemy Unknown	☆ ☆ ☆ ☆ ☆

- [ ] Forza Motorsport 5 ☆☆☆☆☆
- [ ] Rocket League ☆☆☆☆☆
- [ ] The Elder Scrolls: Skyrim ☆☆☆☆☆
- [ ] Sid Meier's Civilization V: The Complete Edition ☆☆☆☆☆
- [ ] Mario Kart 8 ☆☆☆☆☆
- [ ] Trials Evolution ☆☆☆☆☆
- [ ] Halo: Combat Evolved Anniversary ☆☆☆☆☆
- [ ] Katamari Damacy ☆☆☆☆☆
- [ ] Grand Theft Auto V ☆☆☆☆☆
- [ ] Super Metroid ☆☆☆☆☆
- [ ] Her Story ☆☆☆☆☆
- [ ] Kerbal Space Program ☆☆☆☆☆
- [ ] The Secret of Monkey Island: Special Edition ☆☆☆☆☆
- [ ] Surgeon Simulator 2013 ☆☆☆☆☆
- [ ] Dark Souls ☆☆☆☆☆
- [ ] The Sims 3 ☆☆☆☆☆
- [ ] Persona 4 Golden ☆☆☆☆☆
- [ ] Batman: Arkham Asylum ☆☆☆☆☆
- [ ] The Walking Dead ☆☆☆☆☆
- [ ] The Legend of Zelda: Ocarina of Time 3D ☆☆☆☆☆
- [ ] Geometry Wars: Retro Evolved 2 ☆☆☆☆☆
- [ ] Mega Man 2 ☆☆☆☆☆
- [ ] Super Smash Bros. for Wii U ☆☆☆☆☆
- [ ] Final Fantasy VI ☆☆☆☆☆
- [ ] Super Mario Galaxy 2 ☆☆☆☆☆

Author Bio

Chris Watters has been writing about video games for almost a decade. As an integral part of the editorial team at one of the most popular gaming websites, he has previewed and reviewed high-profile games, published numerous in-depth features, and scripted and presented a number of web series. He regularly hosts live stage shows with guests from all over the gaming world at events like E3, PAX, and Comic-Con.

Chris majored in Spanish Lit at Wesleyan University and, while his knowledge of Don Quixote has yet to bear fruit, the language proficiency, analytical acumen, and Super Smash Bros. skills he acquired have been immensely helpful in his professional endeavors.

Chris currently lives in Berkeley with his wife, Jill. He socializes on Twitter at @CTWatters, and wishes he owned a real-life incarnation of Missile, the plucky Pomeranian from Ghost Trick: Phantom Detective.

From the Publishers:

A Quick History of Video Games

It's a Tuesday morning in the 21st century. Whether you're off to work, heading to school, or enjoying a day off at home, odds are you'll play a video game today. Perhaps you'll fit in a few rounds of Candy Crush Saga, or try to outscore your grandmother in Words With Friends. You could be cashing in daily bounties in Destiny, leveling a new character for the next World of Warcraft expansion, or flying through your sixth speed run of Pokémon Red (or Blue). Whatever your game of the moment is, you are one of millions of people around the world who make gaming a part of their daily lives. Video games continue to reach new audiences and evolve in new ways every year, and it's astonishing to think what the future may hold. Indeed, the history of video games is rife with astonishing innovations, and in this appendix, we'll take a look at some of the milestones that led us to where we are today.

The year was 1940. Walt Disney had just released his latest classic, Pinocchio, Robin was introduced as Batman's sidekick, and Al Pacino was born in the Bronx. Just across the East River, the New York World's Fair was taking place, where an engineer by the name of Edward U. Condon displayed an electronic device that played an ancient mathematical game of strategy called Nim. Thousands of people at the fair lined up to test their skills against the computer, and it won over 90% of the games.

A few years later, in 1947, Thomas T. Goldsmith Jr. and Estle Ray Mann file a patent for what they called a "cathode ray tube amusement device." This game used a cathode ray tube that was fastened to an oscilloscope display, allowing players to "fire" an arc representing the trajectory of an artillery shell. The targets? Overlays put onto the circular screen itself.

These games began to inspire other minds and in 1950, Claude Shannon published a paper on how to program a computer to play against a human in chess. Legendary innovator and computer genius Alan Turing worked on a chess program of his own, around the same time as Shannon.

As the 50s rolled on, so did the sophistication and capabilities of computer games. By the end of the decade, there were computer programs for traditional games like Tic-Tac-Toe, Blackjack, Battleship, and in 1958, Tennis. A far cry from that most iconic of digital tennis games, Pong, Tennis for Two was played using an oscilloscope and analog computer, and set up for public demonstration at Brookhaven National Laboratory on Long Island, NY. Though most of these games were ostensibly created as ways to test the limits of computers and their processing capabilities, it's not hard to imagine that those who played them felt the joy of play that has drawn so many to video games over the years.

With the Cold War dominating headlines across the world, it was only a matter of time before burgeoning computer game technology was employed by the military. Among these projects was a creation engineered by the U.S. Defense Department known as STAGE (Simulation of Total Atomic Global Exchange). It predicted that the United States would defeat the Soviet Union in a thermonuclear war and raised the question, is a computer program smart enough to tell its bosses what they want to hear?

However, it wasn't all war games in the 60s. The decade also saw developer creativity flourish. With the help of his brother Paul, John Burgeson runs what is believed to be the first ever baseball computer program on an IBM 1620 computer. Halfway through the decade, football fans got their first taste of gaming glory when a Dartmouth student programmed the first computer football game.

In 1966, Ralph Baer, often named as the inventor of video games, conceptualized the idea of playing a video game using a TV. A year later, he developed the "Brown Box" a prototype that allowed gamers to play tennis. He licensed the technology to Magnavox, and within four years, they released the Odyssey. The Odyssey was the first home video game system, and the world would never be the same.

The 1970s saw space dramas and westerns arrive on the gaming scene, two genres that had long captured the attention of the public and still do to this day. One of these games, Oregon Trail, was a simulation of the perilous journey that pioneers took on when traveling West. This was one of the first games to be distributed nationally, bringing digital dysentery to computer users around the country (in a good way).

As the reach of computer games spread, so did the ambitions of developers. Nolan Bushnell and Al Alcorn of Atari created an arcade table tennis game with the hopes that it would be widely distributed. As the game made its rounds, it developed a reputation for constantly breaking. What ever could have been causing this issue? It turned out that the internal works were being jammed up because so many quarters were being pumped into the machine. And so the legend of Pong was born.

The decade wrapped up with Atari releasing the Atari 2600. This system made gaming come to life in color, and was installed in millions of homes by the end of the century. At the same time, Don Woods's take on the pioneering text-based game, Adventure, initially created by William Crowther in 1975, threw players into a fantasy world of wonders, caves, and treasures. Adventure became the seminal fantasy video game that inspired countless future developers and players.

Atari 2600 four-switch "wood veneer" version, dating from 1980–82.
en.wikipedia.org/wiki/Atari_2600

The 1980s carried the momentum forward and saw the development of many modern gaming icons. The story goes that a missing slice of pizza inspired Toru Iwatani of Namco to create Pac-Man, which went on sale in July of 1980. The in-house version of Pac-Man for Atari 2600 became the first arcade hit to appear on a home device, and the superior Ms. Pac-Man would follow in a couple of years.

Then the real revolution began. Nintendo created a game with a monkey inspired by King Kong and a jumping man. Disney ventured into the world of gaming with Tron. M.U.L.E introduced the idea of co-op games. And in 1984, a Russian mathematician by the name of Alexey Pajitnov created Tetris. However, gaming was not a booming business at the time. Many developers were creating fascinating games, but financial and technological difficulties made widespread adoption an uphill battle.

Nintendo Entertainment System with controller.
en.wikipedia.org/wiki/Nintendo_Entertainment_System

After a significant industry recession in the early 80s, the latter half of the decade saw a resurgence of gaming that we are still enjoying today. This was due largely to that titan of home consoles, the Nintendo Entertainment System. The NES enjoyed widespread success in North America and introduced names like Mario, Zelda, and Metroid into our homes and our hearts. The name "Nintendo" became synonymous with video games, and the stage was set for a series of console competitions to see who could take on the reigning champion of the living room.

North American Super Nintendo
en.wikipedia.org/wiki/Super_Nintendo_
Entertainment_System

Sega Genesis Original Japanese Mega Drive
en.wikipedia.org/wiki/Sega_Genesis

In the early 90s, the Super Nintendo and Sega Genesis squared off. Later in the decade, Sony entered the ring as their PlayStation went up against the Nintendo 64 and the Sega Saturn. All the while, personal computers were improving by leaps and bounds, offering some of the best gaming experiences for those who could keep up with the latest tech. Portable game systems and other competitors made for a dizzying array of options compared to previous decades, and the concept of console wars was born.

Nintendo 64 console and grey controller
en.wikipedia.org/wiki/Nintendo_64

PlayStation console with DualShock controller.
en.wikipedia.org/wiki/PlayStation_(console)

Western and Eastern Sega Saturn
en.wikipedia.org/wiki/Sega_Saturn

What is a console war? From a business standpoint, it's just normal, healthy competition for market share. From a consumer standpoint, it often means allying yourself with whatever system you happened to have and asserting its superiority over those that you didn't. Much like sports fans talking smack about whose team is better, console fans lobbed processing statistics and release line-ups back and forth in debates that carry on to this day. The truth underlying all this hubbub was that anyone who could participate in such arguments was incredibly lucky. The horizons of video games were getting broader by the year, and the new century would bring and even bigger array of options.

In the early 2000s, Sony's PlayStation 2 was the most popular console by a wide margin, though Nintendo's Gamecube drew an enthusiastic fanbase. Sega was selling its last home console, the Dreamcast, while Microsoft was selling its first, the Xbox. PC games remained at the forefront of a graphical technology, but this generation brought online play to consoles, which would grow to be a huge draw for players and developers.

Meanwhile, big things were happening on the portable gaming scene. Sony's PlayStation Portable bet on processing power while the Nintendo DS put its focus on a novel control scheme. The two-screen configuration and touchscreen capabilities of the DS were a hit, and its massive popularity presaged Nintendo's later success with another novel control scheme. As mobile phones charted their own meteoric rise, a new market bloomed for games, though it would be a few years yet before mobile gaming would change the video game industry forever.

The late 2000s saw the widespread adoption of high-definition televisions, and new consoles designed for HD gaming brought the vision of console-PC parity closer than ever before (though still quite a ways away). The Nintendo Wii captivated millions with simple motion controls, and though Sony and Microsoft were waging their own war to see who could deliver the best graphics, they still devoted significant resources their own alternate control devices to capture some of Nintendo's massive market.

But with the release of the first iPhone, mobile gaming was set to redefine the term "massive market." Smartphones soon became far more ubiquitous than any console, and game developers were quick to pounce on the opportunity. While the term "gamer" has often been used to refer to people who enjoy console or PC games specifically, the reality is that anyone with a smartphone can get access to a ton of high quality gaming experiences and call themselves as much of a gamer as anyone.

There are worthwhile games almost anywhere you find games these days, and you can find games in a lot of places. The history of gaming can seem long when you look at how far technology has come, but this is still a nascent artistic medium, growing by leaps and bounds every year to reach more people, create more new experiences, and become more interwoven in human culture worldwide. And with virtual reality set to come to market in a big way in 2016, who knows where the future of gaming will lead? If the past is anything to go by, it's going to be very exciting to find out.

— The gamers at Mango Media

Appendix

Spelunky, Derek Yu, Mossmouth

Assassin's Creed II, Ubisoft Montreal.

Dead Space, EA Redwood Shores (now Visceral Games).

The Last of Us Remastered, Naughty Dog.

Portal 2, Valve Corporation.

Mass Effect 2, BioWare.

Gone Home, Fullbright.

Journey, Thatgamecompany.

Red Dead Redemption, Rockstar.

Uncharted 2: Among Thieve, Naughty Dog.

Nidhogg, Mark "Messhof" Essen.

Psychonauts, Double Fine Productions.

Superbrothers: Sword & Sworcery EP, Capybara Games.

Super Meat Boy, Team Meat.

Rock Band 3, Harmonix and Electronic Arts.

The Witcher 3: Wild Hunt, CD Projekt RED.

Super Mario World, Nintendo.

Half-Life 2, Valve Corporation.

God of War III, Santa Monica Studio.

StarCraft II: Wings of Liberty, Blizzard Entertainment.

Minecraft, Markus "Notch" Persson and Mojang.

Tetris, Alexey Pajitnov.

Brothers: A Tale of Two Sons, Starbreeze Studios.

Animal Crossing: New Leaf, Nintendo.

XCOM: Enemy Unknown, Firaxis Games.

Forza Motorsport 5, Turn 10 Studios.

Rocket League, Psyonix.

The Elder Scrolls V: Skyrim, Bethesda Game Studios.

Sid Meier's Civilization V: The Complete Edition, Firaxis Games.

Mario Kart 8, Nintendo.

Trials Evolution, RedLynx.

Halo: Combat Evolved Anniversary, 343 Industries.

Katamari Damacy, Namco.

Grand Theft Auto V, Rockstar.

Super Metroid, Nintendo.

Her Story, Sam Barlow.

Kerbal Space Program, Squad.

The Secret of Monkey Island: Special Edition, LucasArts.

Surgeon Simulator 2013, Bossa Studios.

Dark Souls, FromSoftware.

The Sims 3, The Sims Studio (Maxis).

Persona 4 Golden, Atlus.

Batman Arkham Asylum, Rocksteady Studios.

The Walking Dead, Telltale Games.

The Legend of Zelda: Ocarina of Time 3D, Grezzo and Nintendo.

Geometry Wars: Retro Evolved 2, Bizarre Creations.

Mega Man 2, Capcom.

Super Smash Bros. for Wii U, Sora Ltd. and Bandai Namco Games.

Final Fantasy VI, Square (now Square Enix).

Super Mario Galaxy 2, Nintendo.

Thanks to the Publishers who contributed screenshots.

Additional screenshots provided by:

http://www.gamespot.com

http://www.ign.com